THE WAY OF SILENCE

BROTHER DAVID
STEINDL-RAST

the

way

of

silence

ENGAGING THE SACRED
IN DAILY LIFE

Franciscan
MEDIA
Cincinnati, Ohio

Scripture passages have been taken from *New Revised Standard Version Bible,* copyright ©1989 by the Division of Christian Education of the National Council of the Churches of Christ in the U.S.A., and used by permission. All rights reserved.

Extracts in chapters six and seven from *A Listening Heart: The Spirituality of Sacred Sensuousness* by Brother David Steindl-Rast, rev. ed., © 1999, are used with permission of The Crossroad Publishing Company, www.crossroadpublishing.com. All rights reserved.

Some texts in this work originally appeared in the following periodicals: *Integral Yoga, Praying, Epiphany, The Quest, Warm Wind—The Chinook Learning Community Journal,* and *ReVision: The Journal of Consciousness and Change.*

Cover and book design by Mark Sullivan
Cover image © Len dela Cruz | unsplash.com

LIBRARY OF CONGRESS CATALOGING-IN-PUBLICATION DATA
Names: Steindl-Rast, David, author.
Title: The way of silence : engaging the sacred in daily life / Brother David Steindl-Rast.
Description: Cincinnati : Franciscan Media, 2016.
Identifiers: LCCN 2016002483 | ISBN 9781632530165
Subjects: LCSH: Spiritual life—Catholic Church. | Silence—Religious aspects—Catholic Church. | Spiritual life—Buddhism.
Classification: LCC BX2350.3 .S745 2016 | DDC 248.4/82—dc23
LC record available at http://lccn.loc.gov/2016002483

ISBN 978-1-63253-016-5

Published by Franciscan Media
28 W. Liberty St.
Cincinnati, OH 45202
www.FranciscanMedia.org

Printed in the United States of America.
Printed on acid-free paper.
16 17 18 19 20 5 4 3 2 1

CHAPTER ONE

Learning to Pray in Silence

1

CHAPTER TWO

The Homing Instinct of the Human Heart

17

CHAPTER THREE

The Mystic in All of Us

37

CHAPTER FOUR

Alive in Body, Mind, and Spirit

59

CHAPTER FIVE

Encountering God through the Senses

77

CHAPTER SIX

Cultivating Grateful Joy

89

CHAPTER SEVEN

Attuned to the Dynamic Order of Love

99

CHAPTER EIGHT

Standing on Holy Ground

109

CHAPTER NINE

Our Quest for Ultimate Meaning

119

CHAPTER TEN

The Mystical Core of Organized Religion

129

MEDITATION

"One Is the Human Spirit"

147

SOURCES

153

CHAPTER ONE

Learning to Pray in Silence

There is a negative meaning to silence and a positive one. Negatively, silence means the absence of sound or word. In these pages we focus on its positive meaning. Silence is the matrix from which word is born, the home to which word returns through understanding.... For those who know only the world of words, silence is mere emptiness. But our silent heart knows the paradox: the emptiness of silence is inexhaustibly rich; all the words in the world are merely a trickle of its fullness.

—From *Gratefulness, the Heart of Prayer*

My earliest recollection of formal prayer is this: My grandmother, rosary in hand, resting on her bed after our noonday meal, would let the beads glide through her fingers, silently moving her lips.

When I remember how large her bed loomed from my perspective, I realize I must have still been small. Yet when I asked her to teach me this mysterious game, she did. The stories behind the fifteen mysteries as my grandmother told them to me stayed in my mind and grew in my heart. Like seedlings taking root in good soil, they kept growing and sending out runners. To this day, like an old strawberry patch, they keep bearing fruit.

Some thirty years later, on a different continent, my grandmother was again resting on her bed and I was kneeling next to her; this time, she was dying. My mother also knelt by her mother's deathbed, and together the two of us were reciting from the English breviary the prayers for the dying. Grandmother was in a coma, but she seemed restless. She would raise her left hand a little and let it fall back on the bed, again and again. We could hear the tinkling of the silver rosary wrapped around her wrist. Finally, we caught on. We stopped the psalms and started the sorrowful mysteries of the rosary.

> My Son came with His apostles to the Mount of Olives. There was a garden there that He frequently went to pray: He felt a sadness; a deep, deep sadness. He felt lonely: my Son in His humanity felt a deeper sadness than anyone could ever feel because He was pure of heart: He was sinless. He took His closest friends, Peter whom He was to give charge of the Church, James, and John. John was the one who was going to take care of me after Jesus had risen from the dead. Jesus said to them: "My heart is sorrowful to the point of death: stay here and pray and keep watch while I go and pray by Myself." Jesus went over further to pray: He wanted to pray by Himself. He wanted to pour out His heart to His Father....

At its familiar phrases, grandmother relaxed, and when we came to the mystery of Christ's death on the cross, she peacefully gave her life-breath back to God.

Another childhood memory of mine is connected with the Angelus prayer. All over my native Austria, the chorus of Angelus bells rises from every church steeple at dawn, at high noon, and again before dark in the evening. At school one day when I was in first grade, I stood by an open window on the top floor looking down on what you might call "the campus," for ours was a big, beautiful school built by the Christian Brothers. It was noon. Classes had just finished, and children and teachers streamed out onto the courts and walkways. From so high up, the sight reminded me of an anthill on a hot summer day. Just then, the Angelus bell rang out from the church, and at once, all those busy feet down there stood still. "The angel of the Lord brought the message to Mary...." We had been taught to recite this prayer in silence. Then, the ringing slowed down; one last stroke of a bell and the anthill began swarming again.

Now, so many years later, I still keep that moment of silence at noon. Bells or no bells, I pray the Angelus. I let the silence drop like a pebble into the middle of my day and send its ripples out over its surface in ever-widening circles. That is the Angelus for me: the now of eternity rippling through time.

Hail Mary, full of grace,

The Lord is with Thee;

Blessed art thou among women,

And blessed is the fruit of thy womb, Jesus.

Holy Mary, Mother of God,

Pray for us sinners,

Now and at the hour of our death. Amen.

I'd like to recount one more memory here, the memory of my first encounter with the Jesus Prayer, the Prayer of the Heart, as it is also called. By then, I was older but still a child; twelve, maybe. I was sitting with my mother in our doctor's waiting room, resting my right hand first on one knee, then on the other, then on the armrest of my chair, then on the sill of a window from which I could see only a high hedge and some spider webs. My hand was heavily bandaged, and I had come to have the doctor change those bandages. After I had examined for some time a jar full of live leeches, which country doctors at that time still kept for bloodletting, there wasn't anything else in the bare room to keep me entertained, and I was growing fidgety.

Then my mother said something that surprised me:

"Russian people know the secret of never getting bored." The Olympic Games were my only association with Russians, but if there was a secret method for overcoming boredom, I needed to learn it as soon as possible. Only years later, when I came across the anonymously written classic of Eastern Orthodoxy, *The Way of a Pilgrim*, did I understand my mother's mysterious reference, for that book was a translation from the Russian.

Lord Jesus Christ, have mercy on me, a sinner.

The Way of a Pilgrim did tell me at length about that secret of never getting bored, but my mother had managed to summarize it so simply that it made even more sense to a boy of twelve: "You need only repeat the name of Jesus over and over with every breath. That's all. The name of Jesus will remind you of so many good stories that you will never find the time long." I tried it and it works.

Boredom, as it turned out, would never be a problem in my life anyway—rather the contrary. Later, in fact, when the Jesus Prayer became my steady form of praying, I came to think of it more as an anchor that keeps me grounded when life is anything but boring. To borrow a phrase from the Roman Missal, the Jesus Prayer keeps my heart "anchored in lasting joy."

After I read *The Way of a Pilgrim*, I made myself a ring of wooden beads that I move, one bead at a time, as I repeat the Jesus Prayer. This movement of my fingers has become so linked with that prayer that I can keep it going with the help of my prayer-ring, even while I am reading or talking with someone. It goes on like background music, not in the foreground of my awareness and yet heard at all times.

The wording I've come to find most helpful is "Lord Jesus, mercy!" The Russian Pilgrim used that longer form, and I have experimented with various versions, but this one suits me best.

Most of the time it expresses my gratefulness: As I face a given situation and take it all in, I see this given reality as one facet of God's ultimate gift, which is summed up in the name of Jesus. Then, breathing out, I say the second half of the prayer, and the sense is: "Oh, with what mercy you are showering me, moment by moment!" Sometimes, of course, "Mercy!" can also be my cry for help, say, when I am dead tired and have to go on to meet a deadline, or when I am reading about the destruction of rainforests, or of the tens of thousands of children who starve to death every twenty-four hours on this planet of plenty. "Mercy!" I sigh, "Mercy!"

The Jesus Prayer has become so connected with my breathing in and breathing out that it flows spontaneously much of the time. Sometimes, while I am falling asleep, the prayer goes on until it melds into the deep breathing of sleep.

The rosary, the Angelus, the Jesus Prayer—these are some of the formal prayers I find most nourishing. They are by no means the only ones, merely the ones most easily described. How could I ever begin to tell you what the monastic hours of prayer mean to me? My small book about them, *Music of Silence*, tries to show how not only monks but anyone in any walk of life can enter into those times of day at which time itself prays. I find the Lord's Prayer and the Creed inexhaustible, too; I'd have to write a whole book about each of them.

Yet, here we are still in the realm of formal prayer, and formal prayer is like a little bucket from which a toddler scoops up and pours out, scoops up and pours out, time and again, water from the ocean of prayer.

Informal prayerfulness is the rich, black humus in which formal prayers grow. We cannot separate (formal) prayers from (informal) prayer. We must, however, distinguish between the two and focus for a moment on prayer as an inner attitude rather than an external form of praying. When I do this, I find myself gliding in and out of three attitudes of praying so different from one another that I think of them as altogether different worlds of prayer.

My key to the first of those inner worlds I call Word. By this I don't mean any particular word or words but rather the discovery that any thing, any person, any situation is a word addressed to me by God. Not that I always catch on to the message, but I know I will get it if I listen deeply with the ears of my heart. St. Benedict calls this deep, willing listening "obedience." We often think of obedience as compliance with a command. But this would make God some sort of exalted drill sergeant. In my experience, most of the time, God doesn't command. Rather, God sings, and I sing back.

The singing, I mean, can be as jubilant as the red of God-made tomatoes, as the soaring of a kite or the splashing of children in a pool. The singing is my heart's joyous response. But God's singing can also be as heavy as the fragrance of lilies in a funeral home, heavy as the news of a friend's grief. God's singing can be as light as harpsichord music or a spring outing, as sad as the howling of a night train or the evening news. It can be cheerful, enchanting, challenging, amusing. In everything we experience we can hear God singing, if we listen attentively.

Our heart is a highly sensitive receiver; it can listen through all our senses. Whatever we hear, but also whatever we see, taste, touch, or smell, vibrates deep down with God's song. To resonate with this song in gratefulness is what I call singing back. This attitude of prayer has given great joy to all my senses and to my heart.

A completely different inner world of prayer where I also feel at home is one to which silence opens the door—silence, not only as perceived by the ears, but also a quietness of the heart, a lucid stillness inside, like the stillness of a windless midwinter day. This silence is brilliant with sunlight as on virgin snow, the kind of day I remember from my childhood in the Austrian Alps. Or it's like the silence between a lightning flash and the thunder crash that follows, the moment in which you hold your breath. On an island in Maine I once found tidal pools on the granite shore with water so still and clear I could see the fine fibrils of sea anemones on the bottom, waving like festive streamers. Still more limpid is the inner space to which silence is the key. I don't always find that key, but when I do, I simply enter. Just to be there is prayer.

To a third inner world, action is the key, loving action. There surely is a world of difference between the prayer of action and that of silence or word. Here it is not by listening and responding, not by diving down into silence, but by acting, by doing, that I communicate with God. Whatever I can do lovingly can become prayer of action.

Nor is it necessary that I explicitly think of God while working or playing. Sometimes this would hardly be possible. While proofreading a manuscript, I better keep my mind on the text, not on God. If my mind is torn between the two, the typos will slip through like little fish through a torn net. God will be present precisely in the loving attention I give to the work entrusted to me. By giving myself fully and lovingly to that work, I give myself fully to God. This happens not only in work but also in play, say, in bird-watching or in watching a good movie. God must be enjoying it in me, when I am enjoying it in God. Is not this communion the essence of praying?

One of the gifts in my life for which I am most grateful is the way I was taught about the Blessed Trinity. Others have told me that, early on, they got the message that God's Trinity is a mystery we could never fathom, so they draw the conclusion, why bother? When I was told of this mystery, it was always in a tone that invited me to explore it—the task not of a lifetime only but of eternal life, life beyond time. My life of prayer has been just this exploration, and it continues to be so. In fact, now in my eighties, I feel I've barely begun.

As far back as I can remember, I had learned to think of God not as far away but as nearer than near. I must have been four or five years old when I came racing from the garden into the kitchen, all out of breath, announcing that I had just seen the Holy Spirit writing something up in heaven. It turned out to have been an advertisement for soap powder, written by a plane so high up in the sky that it looked just like the white dove in the fresco of the Blessed Trinity painted on our church ceiling. About that same time, shortly before Christmas, when Austrian children wait not for Santa but for the Christ Child to bring them presents, I spied one morning a tiny thread of gold lamé on the carpet, and nothing could have convinced me that this was not a golden hair the Christ Child had lost. The chills of awe I felt and the thrill of tender affection are still vivid in my memory.

These childish misapprehensions were nevertheless genuine religious experiences. What was essential to them remains: a sense of God's nearness. Not only did it remain, it kept growing wider and deeper. *Nearness* is too weak a word. From a sermon by our Dominican student chaplain, Father Diego, I soared, ecstatic in the realization that we can know God as triune precisely because we are drawn into the eternal dance of Father, Son, and Holy Spirit. For students in Vienna it is not frivolous to speak of God as dancing. Dancing is serious—not dead-serious, of course, but life-serious. Much later, I learned the hymn about Christ as "Lord of the Dance," set to an old Shaker tune.

I also learned that St. Gregory of Nyssa, way back in the fourth century, had spoken of the relationality of the Blessed Trinity as a Circle Dance; the eternal Son comes forth from the Father and leads us with all of creation in the Holy Spirit back to the Father.

We can speak of this Great Dance also in terms of Word, Silence, and Action: The Logos, the Word of God, comes forth from God's unfathomable silence and returns to God, heavy with harvest in the Spirit that inspires loving action. This Trinitarian perspective helps me understand in ever new ways the "communication with God" that we call prayers—not as a sort of heavenly long-distance call but as the gift of coming ever more alive by sharing in God's life.

Here I come back once more to formal prayer, to the doxology that traditionally concludes the prayers we begin "in the name of the Father and of the Son and of the Holy Spirit." In the concluding doxology, too, we usually connect Father, Son, and Spirit by the word *and*. But I prefer a more ancient version. This more dynamic version suggests our entering into God's life as we pray *to* the Father (Mother and Source of all), *through* the Son (through whom we have communion with God), *in* the Holy Spirit (that Force which comes from God, is God, and leads all things back to the Source in a great dance).

My highest goal in prayer is to enter into that dance through everything I do or think or suffer or say. For that end-without-end I long, whenever I pray: "Glory be to the Father, through the Son, in the Holy Spirit, as it was in the beginning, is now and ever shall be, world without end. Amen."

CHAPTER TWO

The Homing Instinct
of the Human Heart

The key word of the spiritual discipline I follow is "listening." This means a special kind of listening, a listening with one's heart.... In order to listen with my heart, I must return again and again to my heart through a process of centering, through taking things to heart. Listening with my heart I will find meaning.

—From *A Listening Heart*

It is my conviction that at the core of every religious tradition lies an experience that is accessible to all of us, if we open our hearts to it. The heart of every religion is the religion of the heart.

Heart stands here for that core of our being where we are one with ourselves, one with all, one even with the divine ground of our being. *Belonging* is therefore a key word for understanding the heart—the oneness of limitless belonging. A second key word is *meaning*, for the heart is the organ for meaning. As the eye perceives light and the ear sound, the heart perceives meaning. Not in the sense of the meaning of a word that we might look up in a dictionary. Rather, *meaning* as that which we have in mind when we call an experience deeply meaningful. Meaning in this sense is that within which we find rest.

The great teacher concerning the heart in the Christian tradition is St. Augustine. That he was an African may well have something to do with his awareness of soul and heart. Living during the collapse of the Roman Empire from the fourth to the fifth century—the collapse in fact of the known world of his time—he turned inward and discovered the heart. His *Confessions* have been called the first psychological autobiography. In Christian art he is depicted as lifting up a heart in his hand.

"In my heart of hearts," St. Augustine wrote, "God is closer to me than I am to myself." Paradoxically, he also wrote, "restless is our heart until it rests in you, O God." The first of these two quotations expresses our deepest belonging, the second our restless longing for ultimate meaning. What we know at the end of our quest is the meaning of belonging. And the driving force of the spiritual quest is our longing to belong.

In order to check this out more concretely against your own experience, please try to remember now one of your most alive, most awake, most meaningful moments. Psychologists call these moments "peak experiences"; religious parlance speaks of "mystical moments." The mystic experience is an (often sudden) awareness of being one with the Ultimate—a sense of limitless belonging to God, if you wish to use this term. Suddenly, for a brief moment, you feel no longer "left out," as we so often do, no longer orphaned in the universe. It feels like a homecoming to where you belong.

We all have had these moments even if we shy away from calling them mystical. Rightly understood, the mystic is not a special kind of human being; rather, every human being is a special kind of mystic. At least, this is our calling. In peak experiences we glimpse what life could be like if humans were relating to one another and to all there is, not in an atmosphere of alienation, but out of a deep sense of belonging. All of us are challenged by the glimpses we catch in our best moments. Those who rise to that challenge become mystics.

Remember how these glimpses surprise us, when we least expect them? Thomas Merton suddenly felt one with all on a street corner in Louisville, Kentucky, when he had merely set out to go to the dentist. He wrote, "In Louisville, at the corner of Fourth and Walnut, in the center of the shopping district, I was suddenly overwhelmed with the realization that I loved all those people, that they were mine and I theirs, that we could not be alien to one another even though we were total strangers. It was like waking from a dream of separateness, of spurious self-isolation in a special world, the world of renunciation and supposed holiness."[1]

You may have felt this limitless belonging on a mountaintop, or when listening to music. But you may just as likely have been surprised by it when you were stuck in rush-hour traffic or changing your baby's diapers. Whenever it hits us, we know: This is it! This is the answer, as it were, to a question we keep carrying around with us, unable to put it into words and unable to drop it. We may not be able to put the answer into words either—who can put the meaning of a sunrise into words?—but we can rest in it. We have come home. We have found meaning.

Every religious tradition starts from the mystical insight of its (known or unknown) founder. Every one of them has for its highest goal to lead its followers to mystical oneness with the Ultimate.

Attention to our moments of meaning, no matter how fleeting they might be, can lead us even further. They provide us with a brief taste of the nectar, the sweetness

---

1. Thomas Merton, *Conjectures of a Guilty Bystander* (New York: Image, 2009), 153.

in the chalice of all the different religions blossoming like so many flowers in the garden of this world. Our moments of meaning also provide us with a pattern for understanding the differences—and the mutual relationships—between the world's religions. In order to explore this pattern we must look deeper. We need to look carefully at some subtle aspects of your experience to which you may not yet have paid attention.

When we have a meaningful encounter, read or see something deeply meaningful to us, we are apt to say, "This speaks to me." Whatever it is that has meaning for us tells us something, has a message for us; and under this aspect, I call it *Word*. Obviously, we are not talking here about a word from a vocabulary list. Word stands here in the widest sense for anything that embodies its meaning—for the candle, for instance, that you light on a festive table for a meal you share with a friend. It is not difficult for us to see that there must be something that "has" meaning whenever we "find" meaning.

It gets a little more difficult when we turn to a second aspect of every meaningful experience, one to which we tend to pay less attention: *Silence*. An example may help us. We can quite readily distinguish between a mere exchange of words and a meaningful conversation. In a genuine conversation we share something that goes deeper than words: We allow the silence of the heart to come to word. In contrast to an exchange of words, a true dialogue between friends is rather an exchange of silence with silence by means of words.

We have experienced Word and Silence in this sense. By focusing our attention we are able to distinguish them as essential aspects of anything that is meaningful. But there is a third aspect to be explored: *Understanding*. To call something meaningful implies understanding. Without understanding neither Word nor Silence have meaning. What then is understanding? We may think of it as a process, by which Silence comes to word and Word, by being understood, returns into Silence.

There is a curious idiom in the American vernacular: when something, say a piece of music or a moving event (Word, that is) becomes profoundly meaningful to us, we might say, "This really takes me..." or "transports me..." or "sends me...." Language gives us a hint here. When Word deeply touches us, it takes us, sends us into action. Paradoxically both are true: Word, when it is understood, comes to rest in Silence; yet, this rest is not inactivity, rather it is a most dynamic doing. Thus, Understanding happens when we listen so readily to the Word that it moves us to action and so leads us back into the Silence out of which it came and into which it returns. It is by doing that we understand.

Since every religious tradition is an expression of the human heart's perennial quest for meaning, the three characteristic aspects of meaning—Word, Silence, and Understanding—will also characterize the world's religions. All three will be present in every tradition, for they are essential for meaning, yet we might expect differences of emphasis. In the primal religions—African or Native American, for instance—our three aspects of meaning are still quite equally emphasized and interwoven with one another as myth, ritual, and right living. But as the Western traditions (Judaism, Christianity, and Islam) and Buddhism and Hinduism grow out of the primal religious matrix, emphasis falls more strongly on Word, Silence, or Understanding respectively, although all three will always play their role in each tradition.

Allow me to start with my own—the Christian tradition—to sketch a (necessarily rough) scheme that might help us to appreciate the diversity of religious traditions and to understand their relationships to each other. It doesn't take much to see how heavily in Christianity—indeed in the whole biblical tradition— the emphasis falls on the Word. God spoke and the world was created. This is a mythical way of expressing the worldview of the Bible: everything that exists can be understood as Word of God. So central is this notion that one might rightly see Judaism, Christianity, and Islam, all three of them, contained as in a seed in the statement "God speaks."

One of the Hasidic tales told by Martin Buber clearly brings out the preeminence of Word in Western religious tradition. Of Rabbi Zusya, one of the great Hasidic mystics, it is said that he was unable to quote the sermons of his teacher. The story explains this serious short- coming in the following way. Rabbi Zusya's teacher was in the habit of beginning his sermons by first reading a passage from Holy Scripture. The teacher would start by unrolling the Torah scroll, saying "God spoke"... and would then begin to read. But at this point—after simply saying "God spoke"—poor Rabbi Zusya had already heard more than he could bear. He would carry on so wildly that they had to lead him out of the synagogue. There he would stand in the hallway or in the woodshed beating the walls and shouting, "God spoke! God spoke!" That was enough for him. Martin Buber suggests that Rabbi Zusya understood the meaning of God's Word more deeply than all those who could quote their teacher's sermons. "For with one word the world is created," he says, "and with one word the world is redeemed."[2]

Where Word is so central, response will be given a high priority: hence, the emphasis on responding to God in the Western tradition of spirituality. "Living by the Word" is a whole world of prayer that springs typically from the biblical faith in God who speaks. And "Living by the Word" implies far more than the idea that God gives the word in the sense of a command and the faithful carry it out. That is merely the moral dimension of it. The full religious dimension implies that we are nourished "by every word that comes forth from the

---

2. See Martin Buber, *Tales of the Hasidim: Early Masters* (New York: Schocken, 1961), 236.

mouth of God." But let us take Word in its widest sense here, too.

Since every thing, every person, every situation comes from the God who speaks, the whole world is Word by which we can live. We need only "taste and see how good God is." We do this with all our senses. Through whatever we taste or touch, smell, hear, or see, God's love can nourish us. For the one creating and redeeming Word is spelled out to us in ever new ways. God who is love, has nothing else to say in all eternity but "I love you!" And God says this in ever new ways through everything that comes into being. And we "eat it all up"; as we might say of a book, "I devoured it, cover to cover." We assimilate this food and it becomes our life. We live in its strength. We become Word.

So strong is this emphasis on Word in Christian spirituality that even some faithful Christians are hardly aware that there are within their own tradition other worlds of prayer to be explored. One of them is known as "Prayer of Silence." Here the Silence itself becomes our prayer. C.S. Lewis is in accord with ancient Christian tradition when he speaks of God as an Abyss of Silence into which we can throw down our minds for ever and ever, and never will we hear an echo coming back. Yet, this silent abyss is paradoxically also the divine womb from which the eternal Word comes forth. As an early Christian saying puts it: "Those who can hear God's Word can also hear God's Silence." The two are inseparable.

There are more and more Christians today who spontaneously discover the Prayer of Silence. Sometimes they cannot account for their hunger for Silence, their deep desire simply to let themselves down into the quiet depth of God. Unaware that they have found their way into an ancient, timelessly valid realm of Christian prayer, they would be all the more surprised to learn that this could rightly be called the Buddhist dimension of the biblical tradition. Word and Silence are inseparable, as we have said. Just as Word is the core of Western tradition, however, Silence is the core of Buddhism.

Nowhere does this become more obvious than in the account of the Buddha's great wordless sermon. How can there be a sermon without words? The Buddha simply holds up a flower. Only one of his disciples understands, it is said. But how can that one prove without a word that he understood? He smiled, the story tells us. The Buddha smiles back and in the silence between them the tradition is passed on from the Buddha to his first successor, the disciple with the understanding smile. Ever since, we are told, the tradition of Buddhism is passed on in silence. To put it more correctly: What is handed on is Silence.

Not that Buddhists have no sacred Word, but the emphasis is all on the Silence. Their sacred Scriptures are so voluminous, in fact, that it takes a whole day merely to page through them. This is done ritually and with great reverence at least once a year in Buddhist monasteries. And yet, a good Buddhist will say of these Scriptures, "Burn them all!" No one will burn them, of course. That's also quite significant. But just the suggestion to burn them expresses the deep conviction that words must not get in the way of Silence. For the same reason Buddhists will even say, "If you meet the Buddha on the road, kill him!" A Catholic priest I knew caught on to the universal validity of the Buddhist insight and tried to tell his parishioners, "If you meet the Christ, kill him!" His sermon wasn't a complete success—understandably—although the same insight, less emphasized, can also be found in the Gospel according to John, for instance. We simply have to respect the fact that in their quest for meaning Christians are as tenaciously committed to the Word as Buddhists are to the Silence.

Yet, Word and Silence are not opposed to each other. We cannot say this too often. They are two inseparable aspects of religion, of the human quest for meaning. That is why, in spite of all the emphasis on Living by the Word, the Prayer of Silence is equally close to the heart of Christian spirituality and gives Christians—from within, as it were—access to the very core of Buddhism. And since we discovered that, together with Word and Silence, Understanding is another dimension of meaning, we should not be surprised to find a whole other world of Christian prayer focused on understanding. The technical term for it is "Contemplation in Action," but it could as appropriately be named Prayer of Understanding.

Contemplation in the biblical tradition is exemplified in Moses. Moses ascends the mountain to spend forty days and forty nights in the presence of God. There he is shown the vision of the temple. Coming down from the mountain, he brings with him not only the tablets of the Law, the plan according to which the people will be built into a temple of living stones; he brings also the design for the physical temple, the tabernacle, which is to be built exactly "according to the pattern" that was shown to him on the mountain. These two phases of contemplation belong inseparably together: the vision of the pattern and the action of building according to that pattern.

What distinguishes Contemplation in Action is that vision and action take place simultaneously. A teacher who lavishes love on a child understands God who is love simply by loving. The vision of God is given to her in and through her action. How else do we ever understand except by doing? As the saying goes: "I heard and I forgot; I saw and I remembered; I did and I understood." This is why we could call Contemplation in Action the Prayer of Understanding.

"Yoga is understanding," says Swami Venkatesananda with deep insight into what makes Hinduism tick. Just as Jews, Christians, and Muslims in their quest for meaning focus on Word and Buddhists on Silence, so Hindus focus on Understanding. Remember what we said about Understanding as the process by which Silence comes to Word and Word finds home into Silence. This gives us a clue to the central intuition of Hinduism: Atman is Brahman—God manifest (Word) is God un-manifest (Silence)—and Brahman is Atman—the divine un-manifest (Silence) is the manifest divine (Word). To know that Word is Silence and Silence is Word—distinct without separation, and inseparable, yet without confusion—this is Understanding.

The Sanskrit word *Yoga* and the English word *yoke* come from the same linguistic root, meaning "to join." Yoga in all its different forms—service, insight, devotion, and so on—is the action that yokes together Word and Silence by Understanding. And Hinduism knows that this Understanding comes only through doing. In the Bhagavad-Gita Prince Arjuna is confronted with a conundrum he cannot possibly unravel. Fate has placed him in a position where it is his duty to fight a just but cruel battle against his kinsmen and friends. How can a peace-loving prince make sense of this situation? The god Vishnu, disguised as Krishna, Arjuna's charioteer, can give him only this advice: Do your duty and in the doing you will understand.

Consider another example. We may read volumes and volumes on the art of swimming, yet we'll never understand what swimming is like unless we get wet. So we may read all the books ever written on the love of God and never understand loving unless we love. Countless loving people practice Contemplation in Action without having ever come across its name. What does it matter? By loving they understand God's love from within. Just as the Prayer of Silence may be called the Buddhist dimension of Christian spirituality, so Contemplation in Action is its Hindu dimension.

Admittedly, all this is presented from my own perspective, which is a Christian one. But what other option do I have? If I try to be completely detached from my own religious quest for meaning, I have lost touch with the very reality I want to investigate. I would be like the boy who takes his tooth, after the dentist pulled it out, puts some sugar on it and wants to watch how it hurts. One cannot understand pain from the outside, nor joy, nor life, nor live religion. There is nothing wrong with speaking from inside of one tradition, as long as we do not absolutize our particular perspective, but see it in its relationship to all others.

Remember what we said earlier about our peak moments, our glimpses of meaning, and our spontaneous exclamation, "This is it!" The Christian perspective betrays itself by emphasizing the first word of this little sentence: *This* is it! Enthusiasm for the discovery that "God speaks," that everything is Word of God, makes us exclaim again and again, "*This* is it!" and "This is it," whenever we are struck by another Word that reveals meaning. Not so Buddhism. Buddhism in turn is struck by the one Silence that comes to Word in so great a multitude and variety of words. "This is *it*," Buddhism exclaims; and this and this and this, every one of all these words, is always *it*, is always the one Silence. We need Hinduism to remind us that what really matters is that this *is* it—that Word *is* Silence and Silence *is* Word—therein lies true Understanding. The perspectives complement one another.

By appreciating other perspectives we learn to broaden our own, without losing it. In fact, our understanding of our own tradition is likely to deepen through contact with others. Christians, for instance, may see the mystery of the triune God reflected in the pattern of Word, Silence, and Understanding. God, whom Jesus calls "Father," can also be understood as that motherly womb of Silence from which the eternal Word is born, before all time, as by God's self-understanding the Silence comes to Word. The Word, the Son, in turn, obediently carries out the Father's will and in doing so returns to God through that Understanding which is perfect love, the Holy Spirit.

Remember the metaphor of St. Gregory of Nyssa for the relationality of the Trinity. In fact, from all of the Cappadocian Fathers, the great theologians of the fourth century, down to the Shakers in the nineteenth century, Christian tradition has conceived these inner-trinitarian relationships as a great Circle Dance. Christ, the great leader of the cosmic dance, leapt from the heavenly throne, "when all things were in deep silence," and, dancing, leads all creation in the power of the Holy Spirit back to God.

CHAPTER THREE

The Mystic in All of Us

When religious traditions speak of the divine life within us, they refer, implicitly at least, to our high points of wakeful awareness, to our mystical experiences. Yes, let us not shy away from that thought. We are all mystics.

—From *Gratefulness, the Heart of Prayer*

The monk in us is very closely related to the child in us or, if you want, to the mystic in us—and we are all meant to be mystics. We do a great disservice to mystics by putting them up on a pedestal and thinking of them as a special kind of human being. The truth is that every human being is a special kind of mystic, and that creates a tremendous challenge for each one of us to become precisely that mystic we are meant to be. Here, I'm taking mysticism in the strictest sense as the experience of communion with Ultimate Reality. All of us are certainly called to experience this communion. And there's no one and never will be anyone and never has been anyone who can experience Ultimate Reality in the same way in which you can experience it. Therefore, you are called to be that special kind of mystic that only you can be.

Now when I say that this has something to do with the child in us, I mean that there is in the child a longing to find a meaning, an openness to meaning which tends to be lost or at least overshadowed by our preoccupation with purposefulness. I should say right at the outset that when I use these two terms, purpose and meaning,

I'm by no means playing off purpose against meaning or meaning against purpose. However, in our time and in our culture we are so preoccupied with purpose that one really has to bend backward and overemphasize the dimension of meaning; otherwise we will be lopsided. So if you find an extraordinary amount of emphasis on meaning, it is only to redress the balance.

In the child there is certainly a tremendous curiosity about how things work and a tremendous thrust toward purposefulness, and that is the only thrust that we tend to develop. The typical circumstance of a child when seen in public these days is one of being dragged along by a long arm, while whoever is dragging the child is saying, "Come on, let's go! We don't have any time. We have to get home (or somewhere else). Don't just stand there. Do something." That's the gist of it. But other cultures—many Native American tribes, for example— had an entirely different ideal for education: "A well-educated child ought to be able to sit and look when there is nothing to be seen," and "A well-educated child ought to be able to sit and listen when there is nothing to be heard." Now that's very different from our attitude, but it is very congenial to children. That's exactly what they want to do—just stand and look and be totally absorbed in whatever it is that they are looking at or listening to or licking or sucking or playing with in one way or another. And of course we destroy this capacity for openness toward meaning at a very young age; by making them do things and take things in hand, we direct them very exclusively toward the purpose level.

Maybe I should say just a word more about purpose and meaning and the way in which I use these two terms, but I don't want to impose my definitions on you. I'd rather invite you to think about a situation in which you have to carry out a particular purpose and see what the inner dynamics are and then compare this with a situation in which something becomes meaningful to you. When you have to accomplish a particular purpose, the main thing is that you have to take things in hand. If you don't know what it's all about, somebody has to show you the ropes, as we say, so you know how to handle the thing. You have to take things in hand, to handle the matter, to come to grips with the situation, to keep things under control—otherwise you are never quite sure that you are going to accomplish your purpose. All this is very important for dealing with the situation in which a particular purpose has to be accomplished.

Now think of a situation in which something becomes meaningful to you. What is there to grasp? What is there to keep under control? That is not the idea. You will find yourself using expressions in which you are perfectly passive or at least more passive. "Responsive" is really the word, but you are more passive than in a situation in which you are accomplishing a purpose. You will say, "This really did something to me." Now you are not the one that keeps things under control and handles them and manipulates them; instead the experience does something to you. "It really touched me," or if it is very strong, "It hit me over the head!" or, "It swept me off my feet!"—something like that. That's when something becomes meaningful to you. So what really happens is that you give yourself to it, and in that moment, it, whatever it may be, reveals its meaning to you. Again let me stress, this is not an either/or proposition. The two have to go together, but certainly in order to find meaning in our purposeful activities we have to learn to open ourselves, to give ourselves to what we are doing. And that is typically the attitude that the child takes.

Now let me go on in greater depth to what Abraham Maslow called "peak experiences," those moments in which meaning reveals itself to us—and we know it. In order to say more about this, it is again necessary that I don't talk about something that's unrelated to your own experience, particularly since the peak experience in its matter, in its content, is so very evasive. In order to be able to speak about it at all, we'd either have to have a poetry session or a music session or something like that.

The term "peak experience" is a well-chosen term suggesting, for one thing, that it is somewhat elevated above your normal experience. It is a moment in which you are somehow high, or at any rate higher than at other moments. It is a moment, although it may last quite some time; even then that long time, say an hour or so, appears as a moment. It is always experienced as a point in time, just as the peak of a mountain is always a point. Now this may be a high peak or a low peak; the decisive thing is that it comes to a peak.

So you look over your day or over your life or over any period of time, you see these peaks sticking out, and they are points of an elevated experience, points of an experience of vision, of insight if you want. That is also important to the notion of a peak. When you are up on top of a peak you have a better vision. You can look all around. While you are still going up, part of the vision, part of the horizon, is hidden by the peak you are ascending. But once on the peak, you get an insight into meaning; there's a moment in which meaning really touches you. That is the kind of insight that we are speaking about now. It's not finding a solution to a concrete package of problems; it is simply a moment of limitless insight. You are not setting any limits to your insight.

Try to think now of a moment of this kind and make it very concrete, very specific. No generalities will help us here. It doesn't have to be a gigantic peak—they are very rare in one's life. But an anthill is also a peak, so anything that comes to a peak will do for our purposes. So just try and remember very concretely an experience in which something deeply touched you, an experience in which you were somehow elevated above a normal level. I will make a little pause so that I myself can also think of one, and then we will look a little bit into the structure of these experiences. And, if these experiences are, as it appears to me they are, the epitome of the mystical experience, then even in our little anthill-type peak experiences there will have to be found the typical structure of monastic life, as I will go on to demonstrate. So please try now and focus on that one peak experience.

I said that the content of these experiences is very evasive. You might even have to say, "Gee, nothing really happened." Well, that is a profound insight, because if you allow nothing really to happen, that's the greatest mystical experience. But as you talk about it you will find yourself inclined to use expressions such as, "Oh, I just lost myself. I lost myself when I heard this passage of the music," or, "I just lost myself looking at that little sandpiper running after the waves; as soon as the waves come the sandpiper runs back and then the sandpiper runs after the waves." You lose yourself in such an experience, and after you lose yourself for a little while, you are never quite sure again whether the waves are chasing the sandpiper or whether the sandpiper is chasing the waves or whether anybody is chasing anybody. But

something has happened there and you really lost yourself in it.

PARADOXES IN ANY MYSTICAL EXPERIENCE

1. *I'm carried away and I'm present where I am. I lost
myself and I found myself, truly myself.*

And then, strangely and paradoxically—and this is
exactly what we are aiming at; we are trying to find the
paradoxes that must necessarily be in any mystical experience—you find that you would also say that during this
experience in which you lost yourself you were for once
truly yourself. "That was a moment when I was really
myself, more so than at other times. I was just carried
away." It's a poetic expression. There are certain things
in life that cannot be expressed in any way except poetic
expressions, so these expressions also enter into our
everyday language. But then you find again the paradox,
because about the very same experience of which you
say, "I was carried away,"...you may also think, "I was
more truly in the present than I am at any other time."
Like most of us, most of the time I would have to say
that I am not really fully present where I am. Instead,
I'm 49 percent ahead of myself, just stretching out to

what's going to come, and forty-nine per cent behind myself, hanging on to what has already passed. There's hardly any of me left to be really present. Then something comes along that's practically nothing, that little sandpiper or the rain on the roof, that sweeps me off my feet, and for one split second I'm really present where I am. I'm carried away and I'm present where I am. I lost myself and I found myself, truly myself.

2. *When I am most truly alone I'm one with all.*

I go on to another paradox. I suppose that many of you will have chosen an experience in which you were alone—a moment alone in your room or walking on the beach or out in the woods or maybe on a mountaintop. In one of those experiences you find that even though you were alone—and, paradoxically, not so much in spite of being alone, but because of being so truly alone at that moment—you were united with everything and everybody. If there were no other people around with whom you could feel united, you felt united with the trees, if there were any, or with the rock or with the clouds or with the water or with the stars or with the wind or whatever it was. It felt as if your heart were expanding, as if your being were expanding to embrace everything, as if the barriers were in some way broken down or dissolved and you were one with all. You may check this out by finding in retrospect that you didn't miss any of your friends at the peak of your peak experience. A moment later you may have said, "Gee, I wish that so-and-so could be here and experience this beautiful sunset or could see this or could hear this music." But at the peak of your peak experience, you weren't missing anybody, and the reason is not that you had forgotten them, but that they were there or that you were where they were. Because you were united with all, there was no point in missing anybody. You had reached that center, if you want, of which religious tradition sometimes speaks in which everybody and everything converges.

All right, there is a paradox that when I am most truly alone I'm one with all. You can also turn this around. Some of you may have been thinking of an experience in which part of the peak experience was precisely that you felt one with all in an enormous group of people. Maybe it was a liturgical celebration, maybe a peace march or demonstration, a concert, or a play—some gathering where part of your tremendous enjoyment was that you felt that everybody there was just one heart and one soul and that everybody there was experiencing this same thing. Incidentally, this may not at all be objectively true. You may have been the only one who was really turned on like that, but you experienced it as if everyone were turned on in the same way. But even in this situation we turn the paradox around. When you are the most one with all, you are really alone. You are singled out as if that particular word of the speaker (if it's some lecture that turns you on) were addressed to you personally, and you almost blush. You think to yourself, "Why is he talking about me? Why is he singling me out?" or, "This particular passage of this particular symphony was written for me and it was composed for me and it was performed for me; such a tremendous, lavish performance, and it is all for me, right here." You are singled out; you are perfectly alone. And we come to see that this is no contradiction. When you are really alone you are one with all—even the word *alone* in some way alludes to that. It may just be a mnemonic device to remember this, but there may be more behind it—all one, one with all, truly alone.

3. *To find the answer, you have to drop the question.*
I'd like to draw out a third paradox, which in some respects is the most important one, and see again if it checks out with your own experience. When the peak experience hits you or lifts you up or whatever it does to you, in a flash of insight everything makes sense. Now this is a very different thing from laboriously finding the answer to some problem, which is the usual way we think that finally everything could possibly make sense. We think we'll get the answer to this problem, but the moment we have the answer to this problem, several others arise. So we think, okay, we'll follow this other problem up to its end; we believe that we can hand ourselves along from question to answer, new questions arising to the next answer, and to the next answer, and then finally we might arrive at the final answer. But what finally happens is that this chain is a circle and we go around and around and around; the last answer raises the first question and so it goes on.

In your peak experience, somehow intuitively you become aware of the fact that to find the answer, you have to drop the question. Something knocks you over and for a split second you drop the question, and the moment you drop the question the answer is there. You get the impression that maybe the answer was always trying to get through to you, and the only reason it couldn't get through is that you were so busy asking questions.

Why should this be? Why should this happen in our peak experience? There seems a grotesque disproportion between cause and effect. I was doing nothing but looking at a sandpiper running after the waves and running away from the waves; I was doing nothing but lying awake and listening to the rain drumming on the roof; why should suddenly everything make sense?

There's another way of trying to approach this. You might say, if you really try and check out the experience, that something teases you into saying yes. You see the sandpiper and something in you says a wholehearted yes, or you hear the rain and your whole being says yes to it. It's a special kind of yes; it's an unconditional yes.

And the moment you have said an unconditional yes to any part of reality, you have implicitly said yes to everything; not yes to each specific thing, but yes to everything that otherwise you departmentalize into good and bad and black and white and up and down. You are not distinguishing. You just say yes, and all of a sudden this whole thing falls into a pattern, and you have said yes to the whole pattern.

The third paradox lies at the root of what we call obedience. The first thing that we think of is that you do what somebody else tells you to do. That's a time-honored and very helpful ascetic means toward the end, but to get stuck in this would be totally wrong and totally fruitless. If it is just a matter of replacing my self-will with somebody else's self-will, I would rather have my own self-will; it is much closer to home. The whole idea is to get beyond self-will altogether, because self-will is the one thing that gets between us and listening. All our questioning, all our frantic looking for solutions, is just an expression of our little self-will over and against the totality. The moment I drop that, give it up, the whole comes through to me and gives itself to me. I'm not so intent on grasping it and grabbing it and holding it when I give myself to it.

Obedience means literally a thorough listening. In Latin, *ob audire*, "to obey," means to listen thoroughly or, as the Jewish tradition says, "to bare your ear." The ear locks have to be removed so that you can really listen thoroughly. That's known as obedience in the Old Testament. In many, many forms, in many, many languages, the word for obedience is an intensive form of the word listening—*horchen, ge-horchen; audire, ob-audire*; etc.

In other words, obedience, doing what somebody else tells you, may be used as an ascetic means to get over that self-will, that always having your own ideas and your own little blueprints. It's a means to drop all this and to look at the whole and to praise the whole, as Augustine says. But the decisive thing is to learn to listen, and very often doing somebody else's will can be a hindrance to learning to listen; you just become a marionette pulled on strings. This is very important in the context of finding meaning, the context in which we see the mystical experience. When you find something meaningless you say that it is absurd. But when you say "absurd," you've given yourself away—because the term *absurdus* is the exact opposite to *ob-audiens*. *Absurdus* means absolutely deaf. So if you say something is absurd, you are simply saying, "I am absolutely deaf to what this is going to tell me. The totality is speaking to me and I am absolutely deaf." There is nothing out there that's deaf. You cannot attribute deafness to the source of the sound. You are deaf. You can't hear. So the only alternative that all of us have in any form of life is to replace an absurd attitude with an obedient attitude. It takes a lifetime to get just a little way in this.

What all this boils down to is that there is a lot more to life than just the phenomena. There is a whole dimension of life to which we have to listen with our whole heart, mind-fully, as we say. Mindfulness is necessary to find meaning—and the intellect is not the full mind. The intellect, one has to hasten to say, is an extremely important part of our mind, but it isn't the whole mind. What I mean here when I say "mind" is more what the Bible calls the "heart," what many religious traditions call the "heart." As we saw earlier, the heart is the whole person, not just the seat of our emotions. The kind of heart that we are talking about here is the lover's heart, which says, "I will give you my heart." That doesn't mean I give you part of myself; it means I give myself to you. So when we speak about wholeheartedness, a whole-hearted approach to life, mindfulness, that alone is the attitude through which we give ourselves to meaning.

A technical term that is mostly used in the Catholic tradition and is a good term for this is *recollection*—to be recollected, to live recollectedly. It means the same thing as mindfulness, whole-heartedness, openness to meaning. Recollectedness is concentration without elimination (that is T.S. Eliot's phrase), a paradox, because concentration normally limits. But if you can accomplish concentration without elimination, if you can combine the attitude of focusing on something and yet being totally open without horizons, then you have accomplished what recollection means. Then you have accomplished what all of monastic life in any of its traditions is after—recollected living, mindful living, deliberate living.

Thoreau, when he goes to Walden Pond, says, "I have gone into the woods to live deliberately." That means recollectedly, in this sense. There are many forms of monasticism that are not catalogued or recognized as such, and they may be much more important than the others. The decisive thing by which you will recognize monastic life is that it is recollected life, mindful life, wholehearted life. It is through wholehearted living that meaning flows into our lives. That means that while we are engaged in purpose we keep ourselves open enough to let meaning flow into our lives. We don't get stuck in purpose.

It may help us if we see that work in the narrowest sense is closely related to purpose. Work is that kind of activity that aims at a particular purpose, and when that particular purpose is accomplished the work as work ceases. Over against this is play. Play does not aim at any particular purpose. Play has meaning; play is the blossoming forth of meaning. You work until you have accomplished your purpose. You sweep the floor until it is swept. But you don't sing in order to get a song sung—you sing in order to sing. And you don't dance, as Alan Watts pointed out, to get somewhere; you dance in order to dance. It has all its meaning in itself.

Now we tend to think that the opposite of work is leisure. Leisure is not the opposite of work; play is the opposite of work, if you have to have a polarity like that. And leisure is precisely the bridging of this gap between the two. Leisure is precisely doing your work with the attitude of play. That means putting into your work what is most important about playing, namely, that you do it for its own sake and not only to accomplish a particular purpose. And that means that you have to give it time. Leisure is not a privilege for those who can take time for leisure. Leisure is a virtue. It is the virtue of those who give time to whatever takes time, and give as much time as it deserves, and so work leisurely and find meaning in their work and come fully alive. If we have a strict work mentality we are only half alive. We are like people who only breathe in, and suffocate. It really doesn't make any difference whether you only breathe in or only breathe out; you will suffocate in either case. That is a very good pointer toward the fact that we are not playing off work against play or purpose against meaning. The two have to come together. We have to breathe in and breathe out, and so we keep alive. This is really what we are all after and is what all religion must be about—aliveness.

CHAPTER FOUR

Alive in Body, Mind, and Spirit

Sometimes people get the mistaken notion that spirituality is a separate department of life, the penthouse of existence. But rightly understood, it is a vital awareness that pervades all realms of our being.... Wherever we may come alive, that is the area in which we are spiritual.... To be vital, awake, aware, in all areas of our lives, is the task that is never accomplished, but it remains the goal. Since we all know what it means to be alive in at least one area, we have some sense of what it must mean to be ablaze with the Holy Spirit in all of one's life.

—From *Music of Silence*

The first question we need to ask ourselves is: What do we mean by *spiritual*? That is the decisive question. These are three terms that we deal with: body, mind, and spirit. All three terms are more problematic than we realize when we begin to think about them.

When somebody asks you, "Where's your body?" you can point to it. As very little children you have already learned, "Where is your nose?" and then you put (with great delight from your mother) your finger on your nose, and then on your ears, and so on. We have been trained to know where our body is; we have not been trained sufficiently to realize that our body does not end with our skin.

So body, by and large, is not that much of a problem. Mind is more so, but also not too much, because in everyday parlance we just lump everything together that isn't body, and that's mind. So that's fairly simple; if it's not body, it must be mind.

But when it comes to spirit there are all sorts of ideas in the air, and we have to be very careful. A safe approach with words like that is often to go back to the roots of the word itself. *Spirit* means "life breath" in Latin, Greek, and Hebrew. As far back as we can trace, people speaking about spiritual matters used a term which in everyday parlance means "life breath."

That helps us, because I would suggest that what I mean by spirituality and by spirit is "aliveness." Aliveness is of one piece with life as we know it—with the aliveness that you recognize when you are breathing and when your body is functioning.

But it goes beyond that. This aliveness has degrees. Don't you know people who are more alive than other people? Most of us would say yes: So-and-so is really alive! Well, does so-and-so have a higher heart rate, or a faster pulse? Maybe, maybe not, but that kind of aliveness is not to be measured by your bodily functions. There is something else that we are talking about here. But it is an aliveness.

What kind of aliveness is it? What are we talking about? Interestingly, sooner or later we arrive at the word *mindfulness*. In many spiritual traditions that word has been used, and you see, always then you are speaking about the mind again, but you are not speaking about the mind in its fullness. So this aliveness is a fullness of mind. However, we are immediately in danger of falling into a trap. Mind will then be spiritual, and body will be unspiritual. Many people fall into this trap, and this is a very dangerous trap because with mindfulness —that is, this aliveness—goes something for which we have no word, and which we should call something like "bodifulness." But that suggests to you the opposite of slimness, and is not particularly helpful. What I mean by the word is a full, deep rootedness in our bodies.

Think of mindful people: They are rooted in their bodies. They are alive in their bodies. And it's significant that we don't have a word for that, that we just call it mindful. It indicates that there is something lacking; when a word is lacking in a language, there is some insight lacking—the insight that full aliveness is mindfulness and bodifulness, and it's this full aliveness that we are talking about.

Think about a moment of greatest aliveness in your life, a moment of real mindfulness rooted in the body, a moment in which you were in touch with reality. Those are the degrees to which we are alive and spiritual in this world, the degrees of being in touch with reality.

T.S. Eliot said, "Humankind cannot bear very much reality." But we can stand reality in varying degrees, and the most alive ones of us have managed to bear more reality than the others. And what we want to do is become able to be in touch with reality, all of reality, and not to have to block out certain aspects.

The fuller our mindfulness becomes, and the greater we become alive, the more we realize how inadequate language is. So we have to do something, if we want to talk about it, that heightens language. And what is heightened language? The heightened possibility of language is poetry, and so I would like to share with you a poem by William Butler Yeats which hints at one of those moments. It sets religious experience in a context where you would not expect it.

Most of us have our real religious experiences when and where we least expect them; and in environments where we expect them, we are usually disappointed. This is an autobiographical poem ("Vacillation, IV"), and it happens to Yeats in a London coffee shop. This is how he describes it:

> My fiftieth year had come and gone,
>
> I sat, a solitary man,
>
> In a crowded London shop,
>
> An open book and empty cup
>
> On the marble table-top.
>
> While on the shop and street I gazed
>
> My body of a sudden blazed;
>
> And twenty minutes more or less
>
> It seemed, so great my happiness,
>
> That I was blessed and could bless.

So what happens? He doesn't even say anything about his mind or his thoughts; he probably didn't think a thing at that moment. His body blazed with this vibrant aliveness of mindfulness, which is so much more than thinking. His body blazed! And we have all experienced that, or something similar. He says, "It seemed, so great my happiness, / That I was blessed and could bless." That he receives something that he calls blessed—significantly a religious term—and passes on. So something flows through him, and that is that spirit that flows through him.

T.S. Eliot says in "The Four Quartets," also speaking about a peak experience: "music heard so deeply that it isn't heard at all, but you are the music while the music lasts." You are the music. That means you vibrate with that music, and even though you might just be thinking of some flute music or piano music that you listen to, it's the music of the universe that you are vibrating to. It's the music to which this whole cosmic dance dances, and that flows through you—and that's your religious moment. And in that moment you know that you are one with all. You are the music while the music lasts, simply that.

And that is now the expression of a profound belonging. So when you are looking for your peak experiences, or your religious experiences, as you are scanning your memory, forget about all the other things you have thought here that sidetracked you—like "my body never blazed," or "I don't like music" and all the rest. But the one thing that you cannot dispense with is to ask yourself, "Where did I for one split second know that I belonged, and know it in my bones, that I was one with all, and all was one with me?"

That's the essence, and that is a way of knowing. It's the ultimate way of knowing, not limited to thoughts, not limited to feelings, not limited to any other way of knowing. And that is common sense—common sense in the deepest sense of the word. It is a knowing that goes so deep that it is embodied in our senses and has no limits to its commonness. Everything is included: By your own bliss you know the bliss of everything there is in the world, because in that blissful moment you have reached the heart of the world—spiritual knowledge—if you want, commonsense knowledge. The term *spirit* has been so misused that I would be perfectly happy to drop it completely, declare a moratorium on the word *spirit*, and use always the term *common sense*. In contemporary parlance, that says it much better. It makes sense; it's connected with the body through the senses; it's common, limitlessly common.

And common sense is a basis for doing, a basis for action. In common sense, action and thinking are closely connected. So common sense is more than thinking. It is that vibrating aliveness to the world, in the world, aliveness for the world, for our environment. And it's a knowing through that belonging, and so a basis for doing, because to act in the spirit is to act as people act when they belong together. We all belong together in this "earth household," as Gary Snyder calls it so beautifully, and to live a spiritual life means to act as one acts in one's own house where one belongs.

All morality that was ever developed in any tradition in the world can be reduced to the principle of acting as one acts toward those with whom one belongs. And the differences between the different codes of morality are only the limits that we draw for belonging: "These are the ones toward whom you have to act morally, and the others are 'the others,' outside." And when you really live with common sense, that has no limitations; you live out of a morality that includes everybody, and therefore you behave toward everybody as one behaves when one belongs. That is what Jesus meant when he said "the kingdom of God"—and any other term of that sort that you get from any religious tradition will fit in here.

Common sense rightly understood is authoritative. The question of authority is extremely important in this context of religion and spirituality, but the term authority has to be rightly understood, and it's usually misunderstood in our time. Even when you go to the dictionary, and open it up to the word, you will normally find as the first meaning of authority something like "power to command." That's not the original meaning of authority. The original meaning is "a firm basis for knowing and acting." We use it in that way, too; if we want to know something about our health, we go to a doctor who is an authority. If we want to do some research, we go to an authoritative book. We look for a firm basis for knowing and acting.

And now you can understand how we get the power to command, particularly if you reduce it to a smaller sociological scale in a small community—a family or a tribe or a village. There may be a person who proves over and over again to be a firm basis for knowing and acting. You go to this old woman if you want to know how to heal your wounds—or if you want to know whether we should wage war against this other village or not—and she always gives you the right answer. So now, because she is a firm basis for knowing and acting, you put her in an authority position and give her power to command. That's how it came about, and that's how all our authorities can be traced back to having come about.

But the moment a person is put in authority, they normally do not like to let go of that power, even though they may no longer be a basis for knowing and acting. And that is how we get authoritarian authorities. The real genuine authority is so firm that he or she can afford to build you up; actually that is the only appropriate use for authority, to build up those under authority. The authoritarian authorities do not have this basis, and therefore have to keep everybody down in order to keep themselves up, and that is how you can distinguish. It's the litmus test for distinguishing between authoritarian authority and genuine authority: If they build you up, they are genuine; if they put you down, they are authoritarian. It's very simple.

When you really go back to what Jesus Christ set in motion that is still reverberating through the world, it is an authority crisis. He was the kind of prophet that did not say, "I speak to you in the name of the highest authority, and here I come with authority to you." He always appealed to the authority of God in the hearts of his hearers, and that is how he built them up. That's why people said, "This man speaks with authority, not like our authorities." And that got him into trouble; both the religious and the political authorities had to clamp down on him because anybody who makes people stand on their own two feet is dangerous for those authoritarians. They then put him out of the way, but that kind of spirit, because it is the ultimate spirit, could not be killed, and still goes on today.

One more point I would make: If our aliveness is rooted in the body, what happens when we die? We don't have to wait until we die: What happens when we get decrepit? That's really what most of us are far more afraid of than dying. Dying is probably relatively easy; everybody has at least managed it somehow. But to live with this decrepitness, that's really awful, when body and mind begin to fall asunder, as T.S. Eliot says. What do we do then?

Well, I'm at the age now when one really has to begin to deal with those things. I can only give you some thoughts that I myself use for my own encouragement. I ask myself, for instance, Don't I know people who are very old and physically quite decrepit, and yet who are more alive than I can ever hope to be? In a sense, their aliveness is now no longer dependent on the body.

We have even in nature this image of the fruit: The bud and the blossom and the fruit are very much depending on the tree as they are growing. But then comes the point when the fruit is really ripe, and it just drops off the branch, and has its own life and it has the seed for new life. I don't want to push the parallel too far, but we can see in human beings that this aliveness in the mind is something that is not limited by the body.

You can ask yourself, for instance: When you think of your friend, someone you really love—or think of someone you have never met, who lived hundreds of years ago and means very much to you—if you think of that person, you come alive. That's the kind of aliveness that we're talking about. Now you come alive in every way through something that is removed from you in space and in time, and yet it has this influence on you. You can only reach this friend with your mind right now, and yet that mind connection makes you really alive.

That mind somehow is life-giving also; therefore, I can very well imagine that when this life outgrows this aliveness—outgrows the limitations of the body—when this belonging gets greater and greater, that sense of belonging can no longer be limited to this one little body I have here, and then I have to somehow leave this body behind and all I have is that sense of belonging, but that is beyond time. It's not afterward. I do not expect to go on and on and on. Like before, I'm happy that it's over, that it's a limitation, a conclusion. But there is something beyond life that simply lasts, that simply is, that I have, that belongs to me.

That would be one way of dealing with it. And all these things may seem to many of us to come so much from below, you know, working out and up there. Doesn't this come from above? Haven't we been told that God gives us life from above, and God is life, and so forth? Well, my answer is, I believe that myself, but how do you know?

This intuitional question—how do you know?—
always leads you back to your own experience. What
you don't know from your own experience, you just
don't know. Therefore, you have to start from your
own experience, and my experience tells me that when I
am fully alive, in my best moment of total belonging—
when my body blazes, when I'm totally belonging to
everything—then I also belong to God and to that which
anybody calls God if they use the term correctly, that
ultimate reference point of our belonging. Therefore, in
the spiritual experience, in the peak experience, we have
also the anchorage for our religious experience.

The task is to spiritualize all of life. That means to
make all of life vibrant with life—all of our aspects,
including the body. The important story in the Gospels,
the so-called transfiguration of Jesus, literally is depicted
as the body aglow, this peak experience that is here
projected onto Jesus. And in Christian iconography,
particularly in the East, there are very important rules
that must be followed. To a certain extent the artist is
free; but because the icons, the images in the Eastern
Church, are considered as a fifth gospel—as important as

the Gospels as a message about Jesus—they must not be altered in decisive points. And one of the decisive points about the icon of the transfiguration is that Jesus must stand squarely with both feet on the mountain. And if you think of Raphael's famous "Transfiguration" in the West, he's flying up there in the clouds. That is against Christian tradition; he must stand on the ground. It is this body, here in this world, that is transfigured.

CHAPTER FIVE

Encountering God
through the Senses

Why not start spiritual training with a foot bath? For an experience in which our senses spontaneously spark off a grateful response, a foot bath is not a bad choice. Your heart and your tongue may not yet be ready, but in their own way your toes will start to sing gratefully. Can anyone deny that this is a step in the direction of "life abundant"?

—From *A Listening Heart*

When someone asks me about my personal relationship to God, my first spontaneous reply is a question: What do you mean by *God*? For decades, I have been speaking about religion with people all over the world, and I have learned one thing from this experience: the word *God* ought to be used with utmost caution if we want to avoid misunderstandings. On the other hand, I find far-reaching agreement among human beings, once we reach that mystical core from which all religious traditions spring. Even those who cannot identify themselves with any organized religion are often deeply rooted in mystical experiences. This is where I find my own reference point for the meaning of the term *God*. It needs to be anchored in that mystical awareness upon which all humans agree before they start talking about it.

In my best, my most alive moments—in my mystical moments, if you want—I have a profound sense of belonging. At those moments, I am aware of being truly at home in this universe. I know that I am not an orphan here. There is no longer any doubt in my mind that I belong to this Earth Household, in which each member belongs to all others—bugs to beavers, black-eyed susans to black holes, quarks to quails, lightning to fireflies, humans to hyenas and humus. To say "yes" to this limitless mutual belonging is love. When I speak of God, I mean this kind of love, this great "yes" to belonging. I experience this love at one and the same time as God's "yes" to all that exists (and to me personally) and as my own little "yes" to it all. In saying this "yes" I realize God's very life and love within myself.

But there is more to this "yes" of love than a sense of belonging. There is always also a deep longing. Who has not experienced in love both the longing and the belonging? Paradoxically, these two heighten each other's intensity. The more intimately we belong, the more we long to belong ever more fully. Longing adds a dynamic aspect to our "yes" of love. The fervor of our longing becomes the expression and the very measure of our belonging. Nothing is static here. Everything is in motion with a dynamism that is, moreover, deeply personal.

Where love is genuine, belonging is always mutual. The beloved belongs to the lover, as the lover belongs to the beloved. I belong to this universe and to the divine "Yes" that is its Source, and this belonging is also mutual. This is why I can say "my God"—not in a possessive sense, but in the sense of a loving relatedness. Now, if my deepest belonging is mutual, could my most fervent longing be mutual, too? It must be so. Staggering though it is, what I experience as my longing for God is God's longing for me. One cannot have a personal relationship with an impersonal force. True, I must not project on God the limitations of a person; yet, the Divine Source must have all the perfections of person-hood. Where else would I have gotten them?

It makes sense, then, to speak of a personal relation-ship with God. We are aware of this—dimly at least—in moments in which we are most wakeful, most alive, most truly human. And we can cultivate this relation-ship by cultivating wakefulness, by living our human life to the full.

The Bible expresses these insights in the words, "God speaks." Having been brought up in the biblical tradi-tion, I am comfortable with its language, though I would be reluctant to impose it on anyone else. What matters is that we come to a shared understanding of what this, or any other, language wants to express. "God speaks" is one way of pointing toward my personal relationship with the Divine Source. This relationship can be understood as a dialogue. God speaks, and I am able to answer.

But how does God speak? Through everything there is. Every thing, every person, every situation, is ultimately Word. It tells me something and challenges me to respond. Each moment with all that it contains spells out the great "yes" in a new and unique way. By making my response, moment by moment, word by word, I myself am becoming the Word that God speaks in me and to me and through me.

This is why wakefulness is so preeminent a task. How can I give a full response to this present moment unless I am alert to its message? And how can I be alert unless all my senses are wide awake? God's inexhaustible poetry comes to me in five languages: seeing, hearing, smelling, touching, and tasting. All the rest is interpretation— literary criticism, as it were, not the poetry itself. Poetry resists translation. It can be fully experienced only in its original language. This is all the more true of the divine poetry of sensuousness. How then could I make sense of life if not through my senses?

When and to what do your senses respond most readily? If I ask myself this question, I think immediately of working in the garden. The hermitage where I am privileged to live for the better part of each year has a small garden. For fragrance, I grow jasmine, pineapple mint, sage, thyme, and eight different kinds of lavender. What abundance of delightful smells on so small a patch of ground! And what variety of sounds: spring rain, autumn wind, all year round the birds—mourning dove, blue jay, and wren; the hawk's sharp cry at noon and the owl's hooting at nightfall—the sound the yard-broom makes on gravel, wind chimes, and the creaking garden gate. Who could translate the taste of strawberry or fig into words? What an infinite array of things to touch, from the wet grass under my bare feet in the morning, to the sun-warmed boulders against which I lean when the evening turns cool. My eyes go back and forth between the near and the far: the golden metallic beetle lost among rose petals; the immense expanse of the Pacific, rising from below the cliff on which this hermitage is perched to the far-off horizon where sea and sky meet in mist.

Yes, I admit it. To have a place of solitude like this is an inestimable gift. It makes it easy to let the heart expand, to let the senses wake up, one by one, to come alive with fresh vitality. Yet, whatever our circumstances, we need to somehow set aside a time and a place for this kind of experience. It is a necessity in everyone's life, not a luxury. What comes alive in those moments is more than eyes or ears; our heart listens and rises to respond. Until I attune my senses, my heart remains dull, sleepy, half dead. In the measure to which my heart wakes up, I hear the challenge to rise to my responsibility.

We tend to overlook the close connection between responsiveness and responsibility, between sensuousness and social challenge. Outside and inside are of one piece. As we learn to really look with our eyes, we begin to look with our heart also. We begin to face what we might prefer to overlook, begin to see what is going on in this world of ours. As we learn to listen with our ears, our heart begins to hear the cry of the oppressed.

We might begin to smell that "something is rotten in the state of Denmark." We might sit down at table and taste the sweet and salty tears of the exploited which we import together with coffee and bananas. To be in touch with one's body is to be in touch with the world—that includes the Two-Thirds World and all other areas with which our dull hearts are conveniently out of touch. No wonder that those in power, those interested in maintaining the status quo, look askance at anything that helps people come to their senses.

In my travels I notice how easy it is to lose attentiveness. Over-saturation of our senses tends to dim our alertness. A deluge of sense impressions tends to distract the heart from single-minded attention. This gives me a new appreciation for the hermitage, a fresh understanding of what solitude is all about. The hermit—the hermit in each of us—does not run away from the world, but seeks that Still Point within, where the heartbeat of the world can be heard. All of us—each in a different measure—have need of solitude, because we need to cultivate mindfulness.

How shall we do this in practice? Is there a method for cultivating mindfulness? Yes, there are many methods. The one I have chosen is gratefulness. Gratefulness can be practiced, cultivated, learned. And as we grow in gratefulness, we grow in mindfulness. Before I open my eyes in the morning, I remind myself that I have eyes to see, while millions of my brothers and sisters are blind—most of them on account of conditions that could be improved if our human family would come to its senses and spend its resources reasonably, equitably. If I open my eyes with this thought, chances are that I will be more grateful for the gift of sight and more alert to the needs of those who lack that gift. Before I turn off the light in the evening, I jot down in my pocket calendar one thing for which I have never before been grateful. I have done this for years, and the supply still seems inexhaustible.

Gratefulness brings joy to my life. How could I find joy in what I take for granted? So I stop "taking for granted," and there is no end to the surprises I find. A grateful attitude is a creative one, because, in the final analysis, opportunity is the gift within the gift of every given moment. Mostly this means opportunities to see and hear and smell and touch and taste with pleasure. But once I am in the habit of availing myself of opportunities, I will do so even in unpleasant situations creatively. But most importantly, gratefulness strengthens that sense of belonging which I mentioned at the very beginning.

There is no closer bond than the one which gratefulness celebrates, the bond between giver and thanksgiver. Everything is gift. Grateful living is a celebration of the universal give-and-take of life, a limitless "yes" to belonging.

Can our world survive without it? Whatever the answer, one thing is certain: to say an unconditional "yes" to the mutual belonging of all beings will make this a more joyful world. This is the reason why *Yes* is my favorite synonym for *God*.

CHAPTER SIX

Cultivating Grateful Joy

Everything is a gift. The degree to which we are awake to this truth is a measure of our gratefulness, and gratefulness is a measure of our aliveness.

—From *Jesus and Lao Tzu:*
The Parallel Sayings

Delight in sense experience has often received a bad press. Some have put down sensual enjoyment because they thought this was the proper religious attitude. Jesus did not share this attitude. But then, Jesus was not much concerned with being proper. He showed such zest for life that respectable members of society called him "a glutton and a winebibber" (Matthew 11:19). Their own strait-laced stance appeared to them as the truly religious one. In contrast, the friends of Jesus experienced in his company through all their senses God's liberating presence. In the inflection and modulation of his voice God's message reached their ears. What he said was inseparable from how he said it. As his hands touched their skin, God's caring touched their hearts. From there it was only a small step to the insight that every sensuous experience is at heart a spiritual one, a divine revelation. No matter how we repress this intuition, it is there in every human heart just waiting to be triggered.

God's Good news comes to us humans first and foremost through our senses: "Our message concerns that which was from the beginning. We have heard it; we have seen it with our own eyes; we have looked at it and our hands have touched it: the life-giving Word.... We bear witness to what we have seen and heard...so that your joy may be complete" (1 John 1:1-4).

Joy is the gist of the Christian Good News. Yet, only if we open wide our senses will we be able to drink from the source of this joy. Only then will the Good News prove truly good and ever new.

Common sense tells us there is nothing in our intellect that did not enter through the doors of perception. Our loftiest concepts are rooted in sense experiences. Only by going to their roots can we "dig" great ideas. People who are too fastidious to dirty their hands by coming to grips with concepts at their roots are left with notions that are literally "cut and dried." Cut off from the senses, dry reasoning turns into non-sense.

We must, of course, distinguish between sensuousness and sensuality. The difference is that sensuality gets so wrapped up in sensual pleasure that it never goes on to find full joy. A life rooted in sensuousness thrives. A life entangled in sensuality chokes and withers; it resembles a tangle of roots. Healthy sensuousness rises from root to vine to leaf and fragrant blossom. The sweet scent of honeysuckle in the evening air could not exist without the vine's hidden roots; but now this surpassing fragrance has its own existence. True joy surpasses mere sensuous pleasure. Without ever rejecting our senses we must go beyond them. Sooner or later, our senses wilt and die. True joy lasts....

We humans belong to both realms, the realm of the senses and a realm that goes beyond them. This stretches us. To avoid the tension of this stretching process we are apt to settle for half of our rightful inheritance. Still, our human birth gives us a dual citizenship. Only by claiming both realms as home can we avoid the polarization of our human consciousness. Our noblest task is to make the most of this creative tension. If we neglect what goes beyond our senses, we sink below animals. But if we deny being animals and neglect or reject our senses, we clip the very wings on which we are meant to rise to higher spheres. Unless we claim our dual citizenship and are at home with both angels and beasts we become alienated from both, alienated from what is truly human; we become—in Christopher Fry's apt image, "Like a half-wit angel strapped to the back of a mule."...

As human beings we stand at the crossroads of body and mind, of senses and sense. To hold these opposite poles together in harmony is our existential task. Now and then, someone accomplishes this task and the result shines forth as uniquely human beauty: a body radiant with brightness from beyond the senses; intangible splendor yet fully embodied. The eyes of true lovers are lucid enough to see this beauty in each other; we catch glimpses of it in great masterpieces of the visual arts; a piece of music may express it, or a poem, or a dancer's grace. The Austrian poet Rainer Maria Rilke, who wrote his Duino Elegies and Sonnets to Orpheus in the same year (1922) in which T.S. Eliot wrote The Wasteland, made our standing at the crossroads a central theme of his poetic work....

If you have ever watched a honeybee tussle and tumble about in the silky recesses of a peony blossom you will appreciate an image Rilke uses for our task of translating sense experience into experience that goes beyond the senses. Watch that bee reveling in the fragrance of innumerable purple and white and pink petals until, dusted with golden pollen, it finds the source of nectar hidden at the heart of the flower. Watch how with total absorption of all its senses in this peony world the bee performs what is both vital task and ecstatic play. And then read how the poet understands our own task in this human world:

> Our task is to impress on our whole being this passing, impermanent earth so deeply, so painfully and passionately, that it will rise again—now "invisible"—within us. We are the bees of the invisible. With total absorption, we gather the nectar of the visible into the great golden honeycomb of the invisible.

...From hive to blooming meadow and back home our hearts keep winging their way; from the invisible through the visible and then—heavy with harvest like bees with baggy pants of pollen and bellies bulging with nectar—back home to "the great golden honey-comb of the invisible." This is the pattern of our heart's repeated journeys throughout life and of life's quest as a whole....

Most people's glorious gates of perception creak on rusty hinges. How much of the splendor of life is wasted on us because we plod along half-blind, half-deaf, with all our senses throttled, and numbed by habituation. How much joy is lost on us. How many surprises we miss. It is as if Easter eggs had been hidden under every bush and we were too lazy to look for them. But it need not be so. We are able to stop the advance of dullness like the spread of a disease. We can even reverse the process and initiate healing. We can deliberately pay attention each day to one smell, one sound which we never appreciated before, to one color or shape, one texture, one taste to which we never before paid attention. Try for just one week to dedicate each day to cultivating a different one of your senses. Monday: smell day; Tuesday: taste day; and so on. Since there are two more days in a week than the acknowledged five senses, I suggest you give three days to the much neglected sense of touch.

We long to be in touch with life, to touch and to be touched. Yet, we are also afraid of letting anything "get at us." Afraid of letting life come too close, we keep it at arm's length and don't even realize what fools we are making of ourselves. We are going through life like someone stepping into the shower, carefully keeping the umbrella up. We are holding on to our hats, our tokens of social identity and respectability. Far be it from us to make fools of ourselves! It takes a bit of life experience to realize that our choice is merely between making fools of ourselves either intentionally or unintentionally. By refusing to dare and make fools of ourselves willingly and wisely, we make fools of ourselves foolishly....

Joy goes beyond happiness. Joy is the happiness that does not depend on what happens. It springs from gratefulness. When we begin to take things for granted, we get sucked into boredom. Boredom is deadly. Yet, everything within us longs for "life, life in fullness" (John 10:10). The key to life in fullness is gratefulness.

Try this: Before you open your eyes in the morning, stop and think. Remember that there are millions of blind people in this world. Surely, you will open your eyes more gratefully, even if you'd rather keep them closed a little longer and snooze on. As soon as we stop taking our eyesight for granted, gifts spring into our eyes which we did not even recognize as gifts before. To recognize a gift as gift is the first step towards gratefulness. Since gratefulness is the key to joy, we hold the key to joy, the key to what we most desire, in our own hands....

What we have established here, I hope, is that in a spirituality faithful to Jesus Christ sensuousness is not suspect but sacred. A listening heart recognizes in the throbbing of reality pulsating against all our senses the heartbeat of divine life at the core of all that is real.

CHAPTER SEVEN

Attuned to the Dynamic Order of Love

There is the ecstatic instant, but there is no instant ecstasy. Monastic training is unhurried and down to earth: sweeping, cooking, washing; serving at table or at the altar; reading books or filing library cards; digging, typing, haying, plumbing—but all of this with that affectionate detachment which makes the place where you are the navel of the universe.

—From *A Listening Heart*

In [the Christian] tradition the notion of contemplation hinges on the Latin word *contemplari*. The image and, originally, the reality that stands behind this notion, is that of the Roman augurs, who marked off a particular area in the sky, the *templum*. Originally, templum was not a building on the ground but an area in the skies on which the augurs, professional seers, fixed their eyes in order to find the immutable order according to which matters here below should be arranged. The sacred order of the temple is merely the reflection of the sacred order above. Contemplation consists in the bringing together of the two temples, as the *con* in *contemplari* suggests.

Along with this Roman notion there is the biblical pattern: Moses built the sanctuary exactly according to the vision shown him by God on the mountain. Again and again the Bible stresses the faithful correspondence between the temple on earth and its heavenly exemplar. In this sense, Moses truly fulfills the role of the contemplative. And not by chance: What he attempted and what the augurs attempted spring from the same root. The contemplative gesture is deeply rooted in our heart and in our longing for universal harmony. Through the ages humans have longingly looked up to the harmony and order of the starry universe, attuning their heartbeat to its measured movement.

Measure seems to be the basic meaning of the linguistic root from which stem not only cognates like temperature, temperament, template, and temporality, but, of course, temple and contemplation. To measure one's step by a universal rhythm and thus to bring one's life into harmony with a universal order—this is *contemplatio* in our tradition.

To move in step, one needs to listen; to sight one's course, one needs to look. The monastery is, therefore, conceived as a place where one learns to keep one's eyes and ears open. "Listen!" is the first word of St. Benedict's Rule for Monasteries, and another keyword is "consider!"—literally meaning to lay your course by the stars. St. Benedict, the patriarch of Western monks, wants them to live *apertis oculis* and *attonitis auribus,* with open eyes, and with ears so alert that the silence of God's presence sounds like thunder. This is why a Benedictine monastery is to be a *schola Dominici servitii,* a school in which one learns to attune oneself to ultimate order.

But such an order means nothing rigid. That would be the great danger, that would be the trap into which one could fall, to conceive of ultimate order as static. On the contrary, it is profoundly dynamic; the only image that we can ultimately find for this order is the dance of the spheres. What we are invited to do, what we are to learn in the monastery, professionally, is to listen to that tune, to attune ourselves to that harmony to which the whole universe dances.

St. Augustine expresses the dynamism of order when he says, *"Ordo est amoris,"* which means that order is simply the expression of the love that moves the universe. Dante says this, too, in those beautiful lines from *Paradiso*: *"L'amor che muove il sole è l'altre stelle,"* [which translates roughly as, "The love that moves the sun and the other stars"]. But the fact is that while the rest of the universe moves freely and gracefully in cosmic harmony, we humans don't. It costs us an effort to attune ourselves to the dynamic order of love. At some point it even costs the supreme effort of, yes, making no effort. The obstacle which we must overcome is attachment, even the attachment to our own effort. Asceticism is the professional approach to overcoming attachment in all its forms. Our image of the dance should help us understand it. Detachment, which is merely its negative aspect, frees our movements, helps make us nimble. The positive aspect of asceticism is alertness, wakefulness, aliveness. As we become free to move, we begin to learn the steps; to listen to the music, listen, and respond.

Asceticism (in its negative aspect) may thus be understood as training in detachment for the sake of being in tune with universal harmony (the positive goal). But if this harmony is to be truly universal, it must encompass all of reality. If contemplation aims at "bringing the two temples together," all of reality must become transparent to its innermost luminous structure, and ultimate order must find its expression in space and in time. Asceticism must, therefore, cultivate its own environment, as well as its awareness of space and time, as a form of obedience to the environment as guru.

If I understand it correctly, the word *guru* means "dispeller of darkness." Not in the sense that there is something light and good, and something bad and dark. No, reality is not split in two. Let us understand dispelling of darkness in its symbolic sense as the dispelling of confusion. If it is the guru's function to dispel confusion—beginning with the confusion that there are two parts to reality—the result will be order. Only let us keep in mind that it is the dynamic order of life and love, the mysterious order of the great dance. The various traditions have developed a great variety of forms for learning to put one's life in order—into such order. Prominent among these forms is what we might call an environmental asceticism of space and time.

Both in [my Christian] tradition and in others, asceticism of space, the training in detachment as it relates to any given place, centers on learning to be present where we are. This is the first step: and how often do we fail in it! We are ahead of ourselves or are hanging behind. Part of us is stretching out to a future that is not yet, part is hanging on to a past that is no more. What is left of us is not truly present either. We are here and not here, because we are not awake. To be present where we are means to wake up to this place....

Time is something entirely different in the monastic context from that which a chronometer could measure. Time is not ours.... We claim to have time, gain time, save time; in reality time does not belong to us. It is measured not by the clock, but by when it is time. That is why bells are so important in a monastery. Bells are a great help in getting monks out of bed early. No one [who has ever lived in a monastery] will deny the importance of that. But the really important thing is that in a monastery we do things not when we feel like it, but when it is time. When the bell rings, St. Benedict wants the monk to put down his pen without crossing his *t* or dotting his *i*. Such is the asceticism of time.

There are occasions when it is time for something, whether you like it or not. And if you come only five minutes late, the sun is not going to re-rise for you; it is not going to re-set for you; and noon is not going to come a little later because you turned the clock back. Those are decisive moments, around which the whole monastic day revolves—moments that the bell indicates, not just the arbitrary time of some timetable someone has made up. Let all these bells which you will hear ringing remind you that it is *time,* not *our* time.

The moment we let go of our time, all time is ours. We are beyond time, because we are in the present moment, in the now which transcends time. The now is not in the time. If any of us know what now means we know something that goes beyond time. For certainly the future is not, it has not yet come; and certainly the past is not, it is no more. So we say, "Well, but now is." But, when is the now? Is it in time? How long does this now last? Assign the shortest span of time to the now—you can still divide it in half: one half for the future, one half for the past. Is the dividing line then the now? As long as it remains a span of time, you can divide it again and again, *ad infinitum.* And so we find that in time there is only the seam between a past that is no more and a future that is not yet; and the now is not in time at all. Now is beyond time. And we humans are the only ones who know what now means, because we exist, we "stick out" of time. That's what it means to exist. And all those monastic bells are simply reminders for us: now!—and that's all.

To get through this asceticism of space and time from confusion to order, to harmony of darkness and light—that's what we try to do at the monastery. Of course, we cannot claim to have accomplished it.... We are trying to enter into that asceticism of space and time, to open ourselves to the environment as the dispeller of darkness —that is, confusion—thereby finding peace.

Our Latin tradition defines peace as *tranquillitas ordinis*, the stillness of order. Order is inseparable from silence, but this is a dynamic silence. The tranquility of order is a dynamic tranquility, the stillness of a flame burning in perfect calm, of a wheel spinning so fast that it seems to stand still. Silence in this sense is not only a quality of the environment, but primarily an attitude, an attitude of listening. This is a gift that each of us is invited to give all others: the gift of silence. Let us, then, give one another silence. And let us begin right now.

+++

CHAPTER EIGHT

Standing on Holy Ground

*Surprise is the starting point. Through surprise
our inner eyes are opened to the amazing fact
that everything is gratuitous. Nothing at all can
be taken for granted.... When our intellect learns
to recognize the gift aspect of the world, when
our will learns to acknowledge it, our feelings to
appreciate it, ever wider circles of mindfulness
make our world come alive.*

—From *Gratefulness, the Heart of Prayer*

Some insights of our human heart are so deep that only a story can help us bring them home to ourselves and share them with others. The basic sense of what we call, in abstract terms, "sacramental life" is one of those deep insights. The story I have chosen comes out of the biblical tradition. Yet, the basic insight expressed in it belongs to the common treasure of all religions and will be found in stories from many different traditions in the East as well as in the West.

Moses was keeping the flock of his father-in-law, Jethro, the priest of Midian; he led his flock beyond the wilderness, and came to Horeb, the mountain of God. There the angel of the Lord appeared to him in a flame of fire out of a bush; he looked, and the bush was blazing, yet it was not consumed. Then Moses said, "I must turn aside and look at this great sight, and see why the bush is not burned up." When the Lord saw that he had turned aside to see, God called to him out of the bush, "Moses, Moses!" And he said, "Here I am." Then he said, "Come no closer! Remove the sandals from your feet, for the place on which you are standing is holy

ground." He said further, "I am the God of your
father, the God of Abraham, the God of Isaac, and
the God of Jacob." And Moses hid his face, for he
was afraid to look at God. (Exodus 3:1–6)

Has this story become too familiar to make us still
awestruck? Or can we recover the power of this vision?
A bush ablaze, yet unharmed! It is one of the images
that left a lasting impression on the religious mind
throughout the ages, lasting because reinforced by daily
fresh experience. In its immediate context, the blazing
flame amidst the desert bramble stands for the divine
Presence among God's people; it stands for "the Holy
One of Israel." But in a more general sense the thorn-
bush burning, yet unburnt, is a daily sight—daily, yet
ever amazing—for a heart that sees all things aflame
with divine fire.

How staggering is the paradox that shines from the
Burning Bush becomes clear only when later prophets
translate that image into the formula, "the Holy One
in the midst of you." We must remember that holiness here does not mean moral perfection so much as
God's unimaginable otherness. The paradox bursts

upon us when we encounter that unimaginably other One in the midst of what is most familiar to us.

Two attitudes are apt to blind us to that encounter: worldliness and otherworldliness. Worldliness sees merely the bramble; otherworldliness sees merely the fire. But to see, with the eyes of the heart, one in the midst of the other, that is the secret of sacramentality. We shall never understand that secret as long as we look for it in someone else's report, no matter how exalted the experience reported. That is why I must appeal to your own unique personal encounter with the "Burning Bush." We all have had these experiences, though some people are more alert to them than others, or more ready to admit them.

Let me prime the pump by quoting an account by a friend of mine, Don Johnson, in his book *The Protean Body:*

> I walked out onto a dock in the Gulf of Mexico, I ceased to exist. *I* experienced being a part of the sea breeze, the movement of the water and the fish, the light rays cast by the sun, the colors of the palms and tropical flowers. I had no sense of past

or future. It was not a particularly blissful experience: it was terrifying. It was the kind of ecstatic
experience I'd invested a lot of energy in avoiding.

I did not experience myself as the *same* as the
water, the wind, and the light, but as participating
with them in the same system of movement. We
were all dancing together![3]

"Together" is the key word here. All those rifts and
cracks of separation, polarity, alienation, which we
ordinarily experience are healed in one glance. "Like a
saint's vision of beatitude. Like the veil of things as they
seem drawn back by an unseen hand. For a second you
see.... For a second there is meaning," as Eugene O'Neill
described it in *A Long Day's Journey into Night*.

This is the secret of which you catch sight: everything
has meaning. And one glimpse of that secret makes everything whole. The secret is the secret of sacramentality,
the mystery that God's life is communicated through all
things, just as meaning is communicated through words.
The two belong together, meaning and word, God and

---

3. Don Johnson, *The Protean Body: A Rolfer's View of Human
Flexibility* (New York: Harper & Row, 1977), 129.

the world. The two belong together, without confusion, and inseparable: meaning and word, God and the world. As C.S. Lewis writes in the novel *Perelandra*, "He dwells (all of Him dwells) within the seed of the smallest flower and is not cramped: Deep Heaven is inside Him who is inside the seed and does not distend Him. Blessed be He!"[4]

Eugene O'Neill continues: "For a second you see— and seeing the secret, are the secret!"[5] You are the secret because you are seeing it with the eyes of your heart. No other eyes can see it. But being centered in our heart means being together—with ourselves; together with God, who is always closer to me than I am to myself, together in community with all.

For this reason sacramental life always unfolds in community, together. It is never a private affair, though it is deeply personal. Sacramentality is the secret that in our great Earth Household all communicate to all, in a myriad different ways, the life of the Holy One

4. C.S. Lewis, *Perelandra* (New York: Scribner's, 2003), 176.
5. Eugene O'Neill, *Long Day's Journey into Night* (New Haven: Yale University Press, 2002), 146.

in the midst of us. The many communities, churches, communes, are merely pointers toward that one great family of God, more or less successful models and partial realizations of it. Their celebrations of life are somehow sacraments, because life itself is sacramental.

Rightly understood the sacraments of the Christian churches are not self-contained boxes conveying divine grace. They are focal points of that divine fire which makes all life sacramental. It is hard to imagine someone truly understanding the Lord's Supper, for instance, without having learned to look with the eyes of the heart at the robin gulping down an earthworm to feed her young in the nest. The universal law that life must give its life to feed new life simply mirrors the surpassing mystery that through God's love we have life—God's life—by the very death of God. This mystery of the Eucharist comes into focus whenever a community shares a meal mindfully, gratefully.

Biblical tradition (Jewish, Christian, Islamic) sees with particular clarity that sacramental life is realized in time, in history. This is how the Rabbis put it: unless Moses had been taking care of the sheep, he never would have come upon the Burning Bush. Unless we serve life, in the give and take which this involves on all levels, we shall never discover its sacramental power. That togetherness in which sacramental life is rooted includes the dimensions of time, of history, of struggle, of suffering, of service. Moses not only came upon the Burning Bush in the midst of his daily work as a shepherd, but this vision compelled him to struggle for the liberation of his people.

There is only one condition for seeing life sacramentally: "Take off your shoes!" Realize that the ground on which we stand is holy ground. The act of taking off our shoes is a gesture of thanksgiving and it is through thanksgiving that we enter into sacramental life.

Going barefoot actually helps! There is no more immediate way of getting in touch with reality than direct physical contact. To feel the difference between walking on sand, on grass, on smooth granite warmed by the sun, on the forest floor; to let the pebbles hurt us for a while; to squeeze the mud between our toes. There are so many ways of gratefully touching God's healing power through the earth. Whenever we take off the dullness of being-used-to it, of taking things for granted, life in all its freshness touches us and we see that all life is sacramental. If we could measure our aliveness, surely it is the degree to which we are in touch with the Holy One as the inexhaustible fire in the midst of all things.

CHAPTER NINE

Our Quest for Ultimate Meaning

Our religious experience begins and ends with the heart. It begins with the insight that our heart is restless. A world of things can never fully satisfy its restless quest. Only that no-thing beyond all things that we call meaning gives us rest when we glimpse it. The quest of the human heart for meaning is the heartbeat of every religion.

—From *Gratefulness, the Heart of Prayer*

Happiness and a meaningful life are insepa-rable. You may know people who appear to have whatever good fortune can give and are nevertheless desperately unhappy. And there are others who in the midst of raw misery are deeply at peace and—well, genuinely happy. See if you can find where the difference lies.

When we go deep enough, we find that the happy ones have found the one thing which the others are lacking: meaning in life. But we should not call meaning a "thing." It is, in fact, the one reality in our life which is nothing. Nor should we say that someone has found meaning, as if, once found, meaning could be safely kept for darker days. Meaning must be constantly received, like the light to which we must open our eyes here and now, if we want to see.

An image can help us see how meaning can be nothing, or "no thing." We point, in the West, to a vase or an ash tray and ask: "What is this?" No matter how manifold the answers we receive, they will generally conceive of the thing as a certain material formed in a particular way: glass pressed or blown into a certain shape, clay shaped on a potter's wheel, fired and glazed. Of course. It never occurs to us that someone's bent of mind could be so different that the answer centers with the same directness on the empty space of our vase or dish. Surprise. "Empty space? Is that all?" Well, of course, the emptiness has to be defined by this shape or that. But this is less important. What really matters is the emptiness of the vessel. Isn't this what makes it a vessel? We must admit it, strange as this approach may seem to us; as strange as the "sound of no-sound," to which it is closely related.

Silence too, in this sense, is not the absence of word or sound. It is not characterized by absence but by presence, a presence too great for words. When we have some little joy or pain we are apt to talk about it. When joy or pain grows strong we rejoice or cry. But when bliss or suffering become overpowering—we are silent. Any encounter with mystery is hidden in silence. The very term "mystery" comes from the Greek word, *muein*: "to keep silent" or "close the mouth." Mystery is not an empty emptiness but the incomprehensible Presence that touches us and renders us speechless as it imparts to us meaning.

Only by the tension between word and silence is meaning upheld. (Both "word" and "silence" are taken here in the most comprehensive sense, as two dimensions of all reality.) The moment we relax this tension meaning escapes us: the moment we break the tension meaning is broken. Failing to see the distinction between word and silence—a distinction greater and more basic than any other—would mean relaxing the tension. Yet, pushing the distinction to the point of separation would break the tension. The point is that silence and word are distinguished as well as united by the third dimension of meaning we discussed earlier: that of understanding.

After all, how do we understand? I would say, by allowing the word to lead us into silence until we truly hear the silence in and through the word. But more concretely, how does understanding come about in a dialogue? A true dialogue is more than an exchange of words: the "more" consists in an exchange of silence. This is where understanding comes in. For true understanding it is necessary that the silence within me should come to word and so reach out to you until it touches not only your ear and your brain but your heart, your still point, the core of silence within you. Thus, understanding is communication of silence, with silence, in and through the word.

As soon as we reestablish understanding in its proper place, we have gained a new horizon within which to view the relationship of Christian spirituality to Buddhism and Hinduism. If we can accept that our quest for ultimate meaning is the tap root of all spirituality, and if it is true that Word, Silence, and understanding together constitute the sphere of meaning, we can see the possibility that three different traditions within humanity's quest may focus each on a different one of these three dimensions of meaning. Of course, we are not speaking of three watertight compartments but of dimensions which, though distinguishable, can never be separated from one another. Yet, we have seen that in our own tradition the focus on the Word is so strong that Silence and understanding are almost crowded out of our field of vision: We have to make an effort to rediscover their proper place. Thus we should be able to appreciate that in other traditions Silence or understanding may hold a place of preeminence comparable to the one which the Word holds in our own.

If we now consult the data of comparative religion, we find verified what at first sight would seem too good to be true. Jews, Christians, and Muslims find ultimate meaning in the Word. Buddhists (as we have already briefly indicated) find that ultimate meaning in Silence, in the emptiness which is fullness, in the nothing that gives meaning to everything. In turn, understanding, which yokes together Word and Silence, is then the central preoccupation of Hinduism. Admittedly, this sketchy scheme allows for about as much detail as a stamp-size map of the world. The obvious danger is oversimplification. And yet there are advantages to a reduction of scale. For one thing, we shall be less apt to overlook the forest for the trees.

Hinduism, for instance, is so vast and varied a jungle of religions and philosophies that one cannot blame anyone who despairs of finding a unifying principle behind it all. Yet, if there is one, it is the ever-repeated insight that God manifest is God unmanifest, and God unmanifest is God manifest. This is understanding in

our sense, understanding that the Word is Silence—
Silence comes to itself in the Word; understanding that
the Silence is Word—Word brought home. "God manifest is God unmanifest" is the Hindu parallel to Jesus's
word: "I and the Father are one" (John 10:30). Word
and Silence are one and it is in and through the Spirit of
Understanding that they are one. Hindus have spent five
thousand years or more cultivating, not a theology of the
Holy Spirit (theology belongs to the realm of the Logos,
the Word), but what must take the place of theology
when the Spirit is accorded the place which the Word
holds in our approach. Should this not give us hope that
future encounters with Hinduism may tap new springs
in the depth of our Christian heritage?

In a similar way, Buddhism concentrates on a dimension which belongs to the Word but has been somewhat
neglected in Christian tradition. In what would corre-
spond to a theology of the Father (since theo-logy can
only be about the Father), Silence would have to replace
the medium of the Word. Maybe Buddhists could teach
us something in this field. When Buddhists speak of a
door, they do not mean primarily frame, leaf, and hinges,

as we do, but the empty space. When Christ says, "I am the door" (John 10:9) we are free to take this in the Western-Christian or in the Buddhist sense. Why should the latter be less Christian?

It would fall short of the truth to claim that the great traditions of spirituality are complementary. In fact, it would be wrong to think that they could add up, as it were, to "the real thing." They *are* "the real thing" each one of them. They are not complementary but interdimensional. Each contains each, though with the greatest possible differences in accentuation. Each is, therefore, unique.

Each is, in its own way, superior. And what of the Christian claim to universality? Rightly understood, this is not some sort of colonial imperative: it points toward inner horizons. It makes demands of us Christians, not of others, challenging us to rediscover again and again the neglected dimensions of our own tradition, so as to become truly universal, truly catholic.

Not some theory, but our own experience must be the key to an understanding of the spiritual traditions with which we are confronted. For, if our search for meaning in life is the root of spirituality, and happiness is its fruit, we should be able to gain access to all its forms from the vantage point of our own familiar and very personal moments of happiness.

CHAPTER TEN

The Mystical Core of Organized Religion

In the biblical tradition human faith is the response to divine faithfulness. What we are talking about is not restricted, however, to any particular tradition or creed. It is a universal phenomenon accessible to every human heart. All who follow their senses to the faithful heart of reality find themselves both challenged and encouraged to a faith which all the creeds in the world presuppose as their common matrix.

—From *A Listening Heart*

Mysticism has been democratized in our day. Not so long ago, "real" mystics were those who had visions, levitations, and bilocations—and, most important, were those who had lived in the past. Any contemporary mystic was surely a fake (if not a witch). Today, we realize that extraordinary mystical phenomena have little to do with the essence of mysticism. Of course, genuine mystics had told us this all along; we just wouldn't listen. We've come to understand mysticism as the experience of communion with Ultimate Reality (that is, with "God," if you feel comfortable with this time-honored, but also time-distorted, term).

Many of us experience a sense of communion with Ultimate Reality once in a while. In our best, most alive moments, we feel somehow one with that fundamental whatever-it-is that keeps us all going. Even psychological research suggests that the experience of communion with Ultimate Reality is nearly universal among humans. So we find ourselves officially recognized as bona fide mystics. Some of us even sense the challenge to translate the bliss of universal communion into the nitty-gritty of human community in daily living. That's certainly a step forward.

Like every step forward in life, however, the discovery of mysticism as everyone's inalienable right brings with it a puzzling tension. Those who feel this tension most keenly are people who have long been members of an established religion, with its doctrines, ethical precepts, and rites. They may discover the mystical reality inside the religious establishment or outside of it: either in church or on a mountaintop, while listening to Bach's B-Minor Mass, or while watching a sunset.

In any case, but especially out in nature, those who taste mystical ecstasy may begin to sense a discrepancy between this undeniably religious experience and the forms that normally pass as religious. If the religious pursuit is essentially the human quest for meaning, then these most meaningful moments of human existence must certainly be called "religious." They are, in fact, quickly recognized as the very heart of religion, especially by people who have the good fortune of feeling at home in a religious tradition. And yet, the body of religion doesn't always accept its heart. This can happen in any religious tradition, Eastern or Western. To the establishment, after all, mysticism is suspect. The established religion asks: Why is there a need for absorption in the Cloud of Unknowing when we have spelled out everything so clearly? And isn't that emphasis on personal experience a bit egocentric? Who can be sure that people standing on their own feet won't go their own way? These suspicions gave rise to the famous saying that "myst-i-cism begins with mist, puts the I in the center, and ends in schism."

In every religion, there is this tension between the mystic and the religious establishment. As great a mystic as Jalal ad-Din Muhammad Rumi (1207–1273) attacked his own Muslim establishment:

> When the school and the mosque and the minaret get torn down, then the dervishes can begin their community.

Mansur al-Hallaj (c. 858–922), on the other hand, an earlier Persian mystic, was attacked by that same establishment, tortured, and crucified for his mystical lifestyle and convictions, a persecution not without political overtones. One way or the other, the same plot is acted out repeatedly on the stage of history: every religion seems to begin with mysticism and end up in politics. If we could understand the inner workings of this process, maybe we could deal with the tension between mystical religion and religious establishment in a new way. Maybe we could transform the polarization into a mutually vitalizing polarity. Understanding would certainly make us more compassionate with those caught up on both sides of the struggle.

The question we need to tackle is this: How does one get from mystic experience to an established religion? My one-word answer is: inevitably. What makes the process inevitable is that we do with our mystical experience what we do with every experience, that is, we try to understand it; we opt for or against it; we express our feelings with regard to it. Do this with your mystical experience and you have all the makings of a religion. This can be shown.

Moment by moment, as we experience this and that, our intellect keeps step; it interprets what we perceive. This is especially true when we have one of those deeply meaningful moments: our intellect swoops down upon that mystical experience and starts interpreting it. Religious doctrine begins at this point. There is no religion in the world that doesn't have its doctrine. And there is no religious doctrine that could not ultimately be traced back to its roots in mystical experience— that is, if one had time and patience enough, for those roots can be mighty long and entangled. Even if you said, "My private religion has no doctrine, for I know that my deepest religious awareness cannot be put into words," that would be exactly what we are talking about: an intellectual interpretation of your experience. Your "doctrine" would be a piece of so-called negative (apophatic) theology, found in most religions.

Some of us are more intellectually inclined than others, more likely to interpret experience by thinking it through, but all of us do so to a certain extent. Yet, forming an opinion is not all we do. On the basis of that opinion, we take sides for or against; we desire or reject. Our will does that. As soon as we recognize something as good for us, we cannot help desiring it. That is why we commit ourselves willingly to go after it. The moment we taste the mystical bliss of universal belonging, we say a willing "yes" to it. In this unconditional "yes" lies the root of ethics. And all ethical systems can ultimately be reduced to acting as one acts when one feels a sense of belonging.

It is always the whole human person that interacts with the world, but when the interaction aims at knowing, we speak of the intellect. When desire stands in the foreground, we speak of the will. The intellect sifts out what is true; the will reaches out for what is good. But there is a third dimension to reality: beauty. Our whole being resonates with what is beautiful, like a crystal lampshade that reverberates every time you hit a C-sharp on the piano. Where this feeling of resonance (or, in other situations, dissonance) marks our interaction with the world, we speak of the emotions. How joyfully the emotions reverberate with the beauty of our mystical experience! The more they respond, the more we will celebrate that experience. We may remember the day and the hour and celebrate it year after year. We may go back to the garden bench where the singing of that thrush swept us off our feet. We may never hear the bird again, but a ritual has been established, a kind of pilgrimage has been undertaken to a personal holy place. Ritual, too, is an element of every religion. And every ritual in the world celebrates in one form or another belonging—pointing toward that ultimate belonging we experience in moments of mystical awareness.

The response we give in those moments is always wholehearted. In the heart, at the core of the human person, intellect, will, and emotions still form an integral whole. Yet, once the response of the heart expresses itself in thinking, willing, or feeling, the original wholeness of the response is refracted, or broken. That is why we are never fully satisfied with the expression of those deepest insights, in word or image. Nor is our willing commitment to justice and peace, our yes to belonging, as wholehearted on the practical level as it is in moments of mystical communion. And our feelings often fail to celebrate the beauty that we glimpsed unveiled for a moment, the beauty that continues to shine through the veil of daily reality.

Thus, doctrine, ethics, and ritual bear the mark of our shortcomings, even in these earliest buds of religion. Yet, they fulfill a most important function: they keep us connected, no matter how imperfectly, with the truth, goodness, and beauty that once overwhelmed us. That is the glory of every religion.

As long as all goes well with a religion, then doctrine, ethics, and ritual work like an irrigation system, bringing ever fresh water from the source of mysticism into daily life. Religions differ from each other, as irrigation systems do. There are objective differences: some systems are simply more efficient. But subjective preferences are also important. You tend to like the system you are used to; your familiarity with it makes it more effective for you, no matter what other models may be on the market. Time has an influence on the system: The pipes tend to get rusty and start to leak, or they get clogged up. The flow from the source slows down to a trickle.

Fortunately, I have not yet come across a religion where the system didn't work at all. Unfortunately, however, deterioration begins on the day the system is installed. At first, doctrine is simply the interpretation of mystical reality; it flows from it and leads back to it. But then the intellect begins to interpret that interpretation.

Commentaries on commentaries are piled on top of the original doctrine. With every new interpretation of the previous one, we move farther away from the experiential source. Live doctrine fossilizes into dogmatism.

A similar process inevitably takes place with ethics. At first, moral precepts simply spell out how to translate mystical communion into practical living. The precepts remind us to act as one acts among people who belong together, and so they keep pointing back to our deepest, mystical sense of belonging. The fact that a community will often draw too narrow a circle around itself is a different matter. That's simply an inadequate translation of the original intuition. The circle of mystical communion is all-inclusive.

Because we want to express unchanging commitment to the goodness we glimpsed in mystical moments, we engrave the moral precepts on stone tablets. But in doing so, we make the expression of that commitment unchangeable. When circumstances change and call for a different expression of the same commitment, the dos and don'ts remain stone-engraved and unchangeable. Morality has turned into moralism.

What happens with ritual? At first, as we have seen, it is a true celebration. We celebrate by remembering gratefully. Everything else is optional. The particular event that we celebrate merely triggers that grateful remembrance, a remembrance of those moments in which we were most deeply aware of limitless belonging. As a reminder and renewal of our ultimate connectedness, every celebration has religious overtones, echoes of mystical communion. It is also the reason why, when we celebrate, we want all those who belong to us in a special way to be present. Repetition also is a part of celebration. Every time we celebrate a birthday, for example, that day is enriched by memory upon memory of all previous ones.

But repetition has its dangers, especially for the celebration of religious rituals. Because they are so important, we want to give them the perfect form. And before we know it, we are more concerned with form than with content. When form becomes formalized and content is forgotten, ritual turns into ritualism.

Sad as it is, religion left to itself turns irreligious. Once, in Hawaii, after I had been walking on still-hot volcanic rock, an image for this process occurred to me: the image not of water but of fire. The beginnings of the great religions were like the eruptions of a volcano. There was fire, there was heat, there was light: the light of mystical insight, freshly spelled out in a new teaching; the best of hearts aglow with commitment to a sharing community; and celebration, as fiery as new wine.

The light of doctrine, the glow of ethical commitment, and the fire of ritual celebration were expressions that gushed forth red-hot from the depths of mystical consciousness. But, as that stream of lava flowed down the sides of the mountain, it began to cool off. The farther it got from its origins, the less it looked like fire; it turned into rock. Dogmatism, moralism, ritualism: all are layers of ash deposits and volcanic rock that separate us from the fiery magma deep down below.

But there are fissures and clefts in the igneous rock of the old lava flows; there are hot springs, fumaroles, and geysers; there are even occasional earthquakes and minor eruptions. These represent the great men and women who reformed and renewed religious tradition from within. In one way or another, this is our task, too. Every religion has a mystical core. The challenge is to find access to it and to live in its power. In this sense, every generation of believers is challenged anew to make its religion truly religious.

This is the point where mysticism clashes with the institution. We need religious institutions. If they weren't there, we would create them. Life creates structures. Think of the ingenious constructions life invents to protect its seeds, of all those husks and hulls and pods, the shucks and burrs and capsules found in an autumn hedgerow. Come spring, the new life within cracks these containers (even walnut shells!) and bursts forth. Crust, rind, and chaff split open and are discarded. Our social structures, however, have a tendency to perpetuate themselves. Religious institutions are less likely than seed pods to yield to the new life stirring within. And although life (over and over again) creates structures, structures do not create life.

Those who are closest to the life that created the structures will have the greatest respect for them; they will also be the first ones, however, to demand that structures that no longer support but encumber life must be changed. Those closest to the mystical core of religion will often be uncomfortable agitators within the system. How genuine they are will show itself by their compassionate understanding for those whom they must oppose; after all, mystics come from a realm where "we" and "they" are one.

In some cases, officials of institutional religion are themselves mystics, as was true of Pope John XXIII. These are the men and women who sense when the time has come for the structures to yield to life. They can distinguish between faithfulness to life and faithfulness to the structures that life has created in the past, and they get their priorities right. Rumi did so when he wrote:

> Not until faithfulness
> turns into betrayal
> and betrayal into trust
> can any human being
> become part of the truth.[6]

Note that betrayal—or what is seen as such—is not the last step. There is a further step, in which betrayal turns

---

6. From an unpublished translation, with the kind permission of Coleman Barks and John Moyne whose volume of Rumi translations is entitled *This Longing* (Putney, VT: Threshold, 1988).

into faith. This going out and returning is the journey of the hero; it is the task of us all. Faith (that is, courageous trust) lets go of institutional structures and so finds them on a higher level—again and again. This process is as painful as life, and equally surprising.

One of the great surprises is that the fire of mysticism can melt even the rigor mortis of dogmatism, legalism, and ritualism. By the glance or the touch of those whose hearts are burning, doctrine, ethics, and ritual come aglow with the truth, goodness, and beauty of the original fire. The dead letter comes alive, breathing freedom. "God's writing engraved on the tablets" is what the uninitiated reads in Exodus 32:16. But only the consonants are written in the Hebrew text: (*chrth*). Mystics who happen to be Rabbis look at this word and say: Don't read *charath* (engraved); read *cheruth* (freedom)! God's writing is not "engraved"; it is freedom!

It takes courage and vision to see beyond our present understanding. Children do this all the time, with greater ease than do adults. Saying more than she realized, for example, a schoolgirl once wrote, "Many dead animals of the past changed into fossils while others preferred to be oil." That's what mystics prefer. Alive or dead, they keep religion afire.

"One Is the Human Spirit"

Publisher's note: In October, 1975, on the occasion of the thirtieth anniversary of the founding of the United Nations, leaders from the Hindu, Buddhist, Christian, Muslim, and Jewish faiths assembled to consider the moral and spiritual dimension needed for progress. The final ceremony was held in the U.N.'s Dag Hammarskjöld Auditorium. The speakers for Buddhism, Islam, and Judaism held similar beliefs in the oneness of humankind. The ceremony ended with a meditation under the guidance of Brother David Steindl-Rast.

Sisters and Brothers in the Spirit:

Since we are truly one in heart, we ought to be able to find a common expression of the Spirit who moves us at this moment. But the diversity of our languages tends to divide us. Yet, where the language of words fails, the silent language of gestures helps to express our unity. Using this language, then, let us rise and stand.

Let our rising be the expression that we are rising to this occasion in deep mindfulness of what it signifies.

Let our standing be a mindful gesture: mindful of the ground on which we are standing, the one little plot of land on this earth not belonging to one nation, but to all nations united. It is a very small piece of land, indeed, but it is a symbol of human concord, a symbol of the truth that this poor, mistreated earth belongs to all of us together.

As we stand, then, like plants standing on a good plot of ground, let us sink our roots deep into our hidden unity. Allow yourself to feel what it means to stand and to extend your inner roots.

Rooted in the soil of the heart, let us expose ourselves to the wind of the Spirit, the one Spirit who moves all who let themselves be moved. Let us breathe deeply the breath of the one Spirit.

Let our standing bear witness that we take a stand on common ground.

Let our standing be an expression of reverence for all those who before us have taken a stand for human unity.

Let us stand with reverence on the ground of our common human endeavor, joining all those who stood on this ground, from the first shaper of tools to the engineers of the most complex machines and institutions.

Let us stand with reverence on the common ground of the human quest for meaning, side by side with all who ever stood on this ground in their searching thought, in their celebration of beauty, in their dedicated service.

Let us stand in reverence before all those who on our common ground stood up to be counted, stood up—and were cut down.

Let us remember that to stand up as we have now stood up implies a readiness to lay down one's life for that for which one stands.

Let us stand in awe before those thousands upon thousands—known and unknown—who have laid down their lives for the common cause of our human family.

Let us bow our heads. Let us bow our heads to them.

Let us stand and bow our heads, because we stand under judgment.

We stand under judgment, for "One is the human Spirit." If we are one with the heroes and prophets, we are also one with those who persecuted and killed them. One with the henchmen as we are one with the victims. We all share the glory of human greatness and the shame of human failure.

Allow me to invite you now to focus your mind on the most inhuman act of destruction you can find in your memory. And now take this, together with all human violence, all human greed, injustice, stupidity, hypocrisy, all human misery, and lift it all up, with all the strength of your heart, into the stream of compassion and healing that pulsates through the heart of the world— that center in which all our hearts are one. This is not an easy gesture. It may almost seem too difficult for some of us. But until we can reach and tap with our deepest roots this common source of concord and compassion, we have not yet claimed within our own hearts that oneness that is our common human birthright.

Standing firm, then, in this oneness, let us close our eyes.

Let us close our eyes to bring home to ourselves our blindness as we face the future.

Let us close our eyes to focus our minds on the inner light, our one common light, in whose brightness we shall be able to walk together even in the dark.

Let us close our eyes as a gesture of trust in the guidance of the one Spirit who will move us if we open our hearts.

"One is the human Spirit," but the human Spirit is more than human, because the human heart is unfathomable. Into this depth let us silently sink our roots. There lies our only source of peace.

In a moment, when I will invite you to open again your eyes, I will invite you also to turn in this Spirit to the person next to you with a greeting of peace. Let our celebration culminate and conclude in this gesture, by which we will send one another forth as messengers of peace. Let us do this now.

Peace be with you all!

+ + +

SOURCES

Quotes from these books by Br. David appear at the start of the chapters in the present work.

Gratefulness, the Heart of Prayer: An Approach to Life in Fullness. Mahwah, NJ: Paulist, 1984.

Jesus and Lao Tzu: The Parallel Sayings, edited by Martin Aronson, introduction by Br. David Steindl-Rast. Berkeley, CA: Ulysses, 2002.

A Listening Heart: The Spirituality of Sacred Sensuousness. New York: Crossroad, 1999.

Music of Silence: A Sacred Journey through the Hours of the Day, by David Steindl-Rast and Sharon Lebell. Berkeley, CA: Ulysses, 2001.

About the Author

David Steindl-Rast is an Austrian-born Benedictine monk and one of the most influential and beloved spiritual teachers of our time. He has been a monk of Mount Saviour monastery in New York since 1953, dividing his time between monastic life, writing, and worldwide lecturing. He has contributed to a wide range of books and periodicals as well as authored ten books of his own. He is the cofounder of Gratefulness.org, and he was one of the first Roman Catholics to participate in Buddhist-Christian dialogue. He has brought spiritual depth into the lives of countless people through his lectures, workshops, and bestselling books.